the Sonday System 1 ®

Learning To Read

Learning Plan Book

by Arlene Sonday

Winsor Learning, Inc. / St. Paul, MN

Credits

Editor/Compiler: Cindy Guyer
Layout/Design: LaVigne Design, Minneapolis

Copyright © 1997, 2002, 2003, 2004, 2006, 2007, 2008, 2010, 2011, 2012, 2014 Arlene Sonday.
All rights reserved.
6th Edition

This book is the property of Arlene Sonday. Republication or reproduction of any portion of this book without the prior written request and approval of Arlene Sonday is strictly prohibited. All inquiries processed by Winsor Learning, Inc.

Library of Congress 97-62272
ISBN-1-891602-01-2

Manufactured in the United States of America

For additional copies, contact:

Winsor Learning, Inc.
1620 7th Street West
St. Paul, MN 55102
www.winsorlearning.com
1-800-321-7585
sonday@winsorlearning.com

SONDAY SYSTEM 1 LEARNING PLAN
Table of Contents

SONDAY SYSTEM 1 LEARNING PLAN

Check for Knowledge ● PreReading Levels 1-4

ASSESSMENT

For students in grade 1 and older, check for knowledge by going through PreReading Levels 1-4, pages 1-14, to assess student strengths and weaknesses in alphabet knowledge, printing, and phonemic awareness skills. Allow only enough time to determine whether the skill is mastered or if additional instruction is needed; about 3 to 5 minutes for each activity or a total of 30 to 45 minutes. Record the information on the chart below.

Kindergarten children should always begin with PreReading Level 1.

Note: This will take 30–45 minutes

Class, Group, or Student_____

Date_____

PreReading Level	Skills/Activities	Possess Skill/Activity	Needs Instruction
1, Section 1	Alphabet		
1, Section 2	Name Letters		
1, Section 3	Seek and Find Letters		
2, Section 1	Listen to Rhythm		
2, Section 2	Listen to Beginning Sounds		
2, Section 3	Listen to Rhyming Words		
3, Section 1	Practicing Lower Case Letters		
3, Section 2	Practicing Upper Case Letters		
4, Section 1	Combining Words		
4, Section 2	Dividing Words		
4, Section 3	Combine Word Parts		
4, Section 4	Combine Sounds		
4, Section 5	Rearrange Words		

If NO skills are mastered, begin with Level 1,

If SOME skills are mastered, review the mastered skills briefly at each Session while gradually introducing new activities. Spend 2-5 minutes with each activity, alternating PreReading activities in PreReading Levels 1-4 to keep the Session interesting and productive. When working with a group, practice each activity until ALL students are comfortable.

If the student MEETS the goals listed after PreReading Level 4, 'Can We Move On', go on to PreReading Level 5.

* This page may be duplicated.

PreReading Level 1 ● Learning the Alphabet

Written words consist of the sounds of words written in a code which is the alphabet.
Begin learning to read by learning the alphabet.

MATERIALS NEEDED

- Watch Instructional Video ● Music CD ● Word Book ● Alphabet Strips (upper and lower case letters)

CHECK FOR KNOWLEDGE

Ask the Learner to say the alphabet. If it cannot be recited, ask the Learner to sing the alphabet.
- If the Learner cannot sing the alphabet, begin with ① SING AND SAY THE ALPHABET.
- If the Learner can sing the alphabet but cannot say or recite it, begin with ① SING AND SAY THE ALPHABET.
- If the Learner can sing and say the alphabet, go to ② NAME THE LETTERS.

① SING AND SAY THE ALPHABET (auditory)

Together with the Learner,
- Listen to the Alphabet Song on the Music CD.
- Sing the Alphabet Song with the Music CD.
- Sing the Alphabet Song without the CD.
- Say the alphabet without singing it.
- Practice singing and saying the alphabet until it is memorized.
- Read alphabet books to your Learner.

Note: This Alphabet Song separated the sounds of l-m-n-o-p so they can be heard separately.

② NAME THE LETTERS (visual/auditory)

- Turn to the inside front cover of the Word Book and have the Learner say the alphabet, pointing to each letter as it is named.
- Find the Alphabet Strip with upper case (capital) letters.
- Learner names the letters of the alphabet in order pointing to each letter on the Alphabet Strip as it is named.

Option: Magnetic letters provide another way to do this activity.

SONDAY SYSTEM 1 LEARNING PLAN

PreReading Level 1 • Learning the Alphabet

3 SEEK AND FIND LETTERS (visual/auditory/kinesthetic)

3-5 MIN.

- Fold the Alphabet Strip with upper case (capital) letters so that <u>a</u> through <u>g</u> are exposed. Ask,
  - "Find the letter <u>d</u>."
  - "Good! Now point to the letter before the <u>d</u>. What is the name of that letter?"
  - "Point to the letter after the <u>d</u>. What is the name of that letter?"
  - "Find the letter <u>f</u>."
  - "Good! Now point to the letter before the <u>f</u>. What is the name of that letter?"
  - "Point to the letter after the <u>f</u>. What is the name of that letter?"

Repeat this dialogue until all letters have been practiced.
- Add the next segment of the Alphabet Strip so the letters <u>a</u> through <u>n</u> are exposed. This broadens the search.

Repeat the same routine but select random letters from <u>a</u> through <u>n</u>.
- Expose the <u>o</u> through <u>s</u> segment, then the <u>t</u> through <u>z</u> segment.

If your Learner knows many of the lower case (small) letters,
- Repeat ② NAME THE LETTERS and ③ SEEK AND FIND LETTERS using the lower case alphabet inside the back cover of the Word Book and the Alphabet Strip with lower case letters.

Continue to review these activities regularly as you move on to PreReading Level 2.

PreReading Level 2 • Developing Listening Skills

Listening to patterns and reproducing them is an important foundation skill for reading and spelling. Some Learners can "play" with language comfortably while others, especially those who are having trouble learning to read and spell, may need practice with listening games or sound puzzles. In this PreReading Level, begin learning how to "play" with language.

MATERIALS NEEDED

● Watch Instructional Video ● Music CD

REVIEW

As you introduce the new activities in PreReading Level 2, continue to:

● Say and Sing the Alphabet   ● Name the Letters in Sequence   ● Seek and Find Letters

1 LISTEN TO RHYTHM (auditory/kinesthetic)

3 MIN.

● Clap your hands two or three times and ask the Learner to imitate the clapping patterns. You might try

     clap clap — clap
     clap — clap clap

● Increase to four and five claps after the Learner is able to manage three comfortably.
Sounds can be made with other instruments or a variety of noises once the clapping patterns come easily.

● Move on to ② Listen to Beginning Sounds even if this skill has not been mastered.

2 LISTEN TO BEGINNING SOUNDS (auditory)

3 MIN.

Separating the first sound of a word from the rest of the word is the beginning of spelling.

   ● Listen to the Beginning Sounds Song on the Music CD.
   ● Sing it together with and without the CD.
   ● Practice using words that are not in the song. Additional word lists are in the Word Book, page 3.
   ● Ask the Learner to think of words that begin with the sound /s/. Model using the following:

       sun   sand   sing   sign

   ● Ask the Learner to think of words that begin with /m/, /l/, /d/, etc.

Note: The slashes on either side of the letter indicate that the sound of the letter, not the name, is used. Example: /m/

SONDAY SYSTEM 1 LEARNING PLAN

PreReading Level 2 ● *Developing Listening Skills*

 3

LISTEN TO RHYMING WORDS (auditory)

- Listen to the Rhyming Song on the Music CD.
- Sing it together with and without the CD.
- Then say, "Tell me a word that rhymes with 'say'."
  "Tell me a word that rhymes with 'fall'."
  "How many words can we think of that rhyme with 'mat'?"

This can be done in the car, in the kitchen, in a waiting room, or at the beach.
Sets of rhyming words are listed below and on the next page.

Continue to review the activities in PreReading Levels 1 and 2 as you move on to PreReading Level 3.

Rhyming words used in the Rhyming Song on the Music CD

day	may	say	hay	ray	tray	lay	stay
snow	show	blow	bow	low	tow	go	no
my	by	shy	fly	dry	spy	try	high
old	fold	gold	sold	told	hold	bold	cold
pat	rat	hat	mat	sat	gnat	bat	cat
sing	ring	thing	wing	bring	king	sting	zing
candy	dandy	handy	sandy	trusty	rusty	dusty	musty
ringing	singing	bringing	clinging	packing	tracking	cracking	stacking
funny	money	nifty	thrifty	ducky	lucky	farming	charming
mister	sister	tricky	sticky	louder	powder	mitten	kitten

PreReading Level 2 • Developing Listening Skills

3 ## LISTEN TO RHYMING WORDS (CONTINUED)

More rhyming sets to be used with Rhyming Song (Instrumental Version) on the Music CD.

cash	man	pick	feet	or	saw
trash	fan	lick	sweet	pour	raw
flash	ran	tick	seat	bore	claw
dash	tan	click	meet	door	paw
rash	pan	sick	neat	floor	draw
hash	plan	brick	beat	more	jaw
sash	can	stick	sheet	roar	law
bash	van	kick	sleet	store	straw
pass	sink	back	deep	ate	ringing
grass	wink	rack	leap	bait	singing
class	think	pack	steep	fate	bringing
bass	rink	black	creep	plate	stinging
brass	blink	sack	heap	slate	clinging
lass	drink	tack	beep	skate	winging
mass	pink	crack	sleep	wait	flinging
glass	stink	jack	keep	late	swinging
ball	sank	park	speed	torn	packing
wall	bank	dark	need	born	tacking
tall	rank	bark	greed	morn	cracking
call	thank	shark	bleed	corn	stacking
doll	drank	lark	feed	worn	lacking
mall	tank	mark	breed	thorn	backing
fall	plank	ark	weed	horn	snacking
hall	prank	spark	seed	sworn	tracking
find	sit	port	hair	bean	quicker
mind	bit	fort	bear	clean	sticker
blind	fit	sort	care	seen	clicker
grind	hit	sport	wear	queen	picker
bind	pit	short	air	green	ticker
kind	slit	court	dare	mean	kicker
wind	mitt	snort	fair	jean	sicker
hind	grit	tort	rare	teen	slicker

PreReading Level 3 • Printing Letters

Forming the letters of the alphabet is the first step in writing. Printing letters while saying the names and/or sounds aloud completes the seeing, hearing, feeling practice that cements learning.

MATERIALS NEEDED

- Watch Instructional Video • Music CD • Word Book • Letter Tactile Cards • White Glue • Sand Tray • Printing Practice Pages
- Transparency with Washable Pen • Paper Clips • Paper and Pencil

REVIEW

As you introduce the new activities in PreReading Level 3, continue to:

- Say and Sing the Alphabet
- Play with Rhythm
- Name the Letters in Sequence
- Play with Beginning Sounds
- Seek and Find Letters
- Play with Rhyming Words

CHECK FOR KNOWLEDGE

Ask the Learner to write the alphabet. Don't be concerned about mixed upper case (capital) and lower case (small) letters at this point. If some letters are skipped, dictate the alphabet and have the Learner write the letters again as they are named. The purpose is to find which letters the Learner can print, which letters are printed properly and which ones need to be learned.

- If the Learner cannot print all of the letters, begin with ① TRACE LETTERS.
- If the Learner can print all of the letters but doesn't use suggested strokes and directional arrows, begin with ① TRACE LETTERS. Using correct strokes will make learning cursive writing easier.
- If the Learner can print all of the letters correctly go on to ③ PRINT LETTERS to practice correct letter formation on paper.

| HELPER'S NOTE | If the Learner is in school and is currently using lower case letters, begin by practicing lower case printing, then teach upper case. If upper case printing has been introduced in school, begin by practicing the capital letters. |

SONDAY SYSTEM 1 LEARNING PLAN

PreReading Level 3 • *Printing Letters*

---

1 TRACE LETTERS

This activity helps the Learner's developing muscles learn the shapes of the letters.

Letter Tactile Cards

- Using two fingers of the writing hand, Learner traces the letters while saying the name of each letter, observing the starting point, the sequence of strokes, and the directional arrows.

Word Book

- Find the upper case (capital) letters inside the front cover of the Word Book or the lower case (small) letters inside the back cover.
- Learner uses two fingers of the writing hand to trace the letters. Remember the starting points and direction of strokes.

HELPERS NOTE	Remember, that Learners using upper case letters should practice them. Learners using lower case should practice lower case letters.

---

2 DRAW LETTERS

Sand Tray

To make a sand tray: Find the plastic tray. Put about 1/4 inch of sand, salt, cornmeal, or rice in the bottom. Learner forms letters in the sand. Shake the sand tray to erase.

- Dictate letters of the alphabet by name.
- Learner repeats the letter name and prints the letter in the sand tray, using starting points and directional strokes practiced.

Other devices for encouraging touch reinforcement for printing letters could include finger paint, shaving cream, a carpet sample, chalkboard with chalk or a wet foam brush, magic slate, or paper with crayons or markers.

5-10 MIN.

3 PRINT LETTERS

Printing Practice Pages

To use Printing Practice Pages: Find the Printing Practice Pages, Transparency and Washable Transparency Pen. By using the washable pen, the practice sheets can be reused.

- Beginning with page 1, Learner practices making downstrokes from the top line and downstrokes from the dotted line.
- Learner practices making circles beginning at the starting point and moving counterclockwise.
- Learner practices formation of letters.

HELPERS NOTE

Proficient printers may practice only those letters that are troublesome and then move on to PreReading Level 4.

Introduce just one new letter at a Session but review all known letters at each Session.
Review may be done using the sand tray or Printing Practice Pages.

The following overview shows the order in which letters will be introduced on the Printing Practice Pages.

HELPERS NOTE

If the Learner is using upper case (capital) letters in school, begin by teaching upper case letters.
If the Learner is using lower case (small) letters in school, begin by teaching lower case letters.

Lower Case Letters

Begin with the short letters that start with a down stroke from the dotted line.

Tall letters begin with a down stroke from the top line, except for <u>t</u> which starts just below the top line.

Using the face of a clock as a model, begin the circle letters at one o'clock.

<u>o</u> begins at twelve o'clock. Note that <u>e</u> has a different starting point.

o e

SONDAY SYSTEM 1 LEARNING PLAN

PreReading Level 3 • *Printing Letters*

③ PRINT LETTERS

Slant letters

v w x y z

Upper Case Letters

Begin with the letters that start with a down stroke from the top line.

L T I H F E D P

R B J K M N U

Using the face of a clock as a model, begin the circle letters at one o'clock.

C G S

O and Q begin at twelve o'clock.

O Q

Slant letters

A V W X Y Z

Continue to review the activities in PreReading Levels 1 through 3 as you move on to PreReading Level 4.

PreReading Level 4● *Playing with Sound Puzzles*

Combining two small words into a compound word provides a foundation for blending sounds together to make words. Dividing words into parts leads to separating words into sounds for spelling. Practice the sound puzzles that make reading and spelling easier.

MATERIALS NEEDED

• Watch Instructional Video • Music CD

REVIEW

As new activities are introduced in PreReading Level 4, continue to:
• Sing and Say the Alphabet
• Play with Rhythm
• Trace Letter Tactile Cards
• Name the Letters in Sequence
• Play with Beginning Sounds
• Draw Letters in Sand Tray
• Seek and Find Letters
• Play with Rhyming Words
• Print Letters on Paper

① COMBINE WORDS (auditory)

2-3 MIN.

• Listen to the Combining Words Song on the Music CD.
• Sing it together. Memorize.
• Use the Combining Words Song (Instrumental Version) to create a new song using the words suggested below.

pop...corn	air...port	hay...stack
pan...cake	Bat...man	bath...tub
air...plane	moon...light	sun...shine

• Practice saying the words instead of singing them so the Learner can combine words without the music.

Say to the Learner,
　　　　"Can you make one word out of 'pop...corn'?"
　　　　"Can you make one word out of 'pan...cake'?"

Additional words are listed under ② DIVIDE WORDS and page 84 of the Word Book.

SONDAY SYSTEM 1 LEARNING PLAN
PreReading Level 4● Playing with Sound Puzzles

② DIVIDE WORDS (auditory)

- Listen to the Dividing Words Song on the Music CD.
- Sing it together. Memorize.
- Using the Dividing Words Song (Instrumental Version), create a new song using the words suggested below.

baseball	raincoat	doorbell
driveway	mailbox	sailboat
cupcake	cowboy	catfish
bedroom	hillside	hotrod

- Practice dividing compound words into parts by saying the words and having the Learner make each word into two words.

Say to the Learner,

"Can you make two words out of 'baseball'?"

"Can you make two words out of 'driveway'?"

Additional words are listed under ① COMBINE WORDS and page 84 of the Word Book.

③ COMBINE WORD PARTS (auditory)

- Learner combines parts of words to make whole words. Watch the video demonstration.

Say to the Learner,

"Can you make a word out of /fla/......(pause)....../sh/?"

"Can you make a word out of /s/......(pause)....../ink/?"

Examples:

brow...n	spee...d	shar...p
shor...t	smar...t	cree...p
crow...d	sma...sh	pun...ch
b...ark	t...ack	f...ill
b...all	f...arm	m...eet
sh...eep	c...ow	th...ing

COMBINE SOUNDS (auditory)

2 MIN.

- Learner combines single sounds to make short, real words.

Say to the Learner,

"Can you make a word out of /m/......(pause)....../ay/?"

"Can you make a word out of /s/......(pause)....../ee/?"

Examples:

m...e	s...ay	sh...e	p...ay
p...ie	m...y	d...ay	t...ie
w...e	sh...ow	m...ow	g...o
l ...ay	d...ie	b...y	l...ow

REARRANGE WORDS (auditory)

3 MIN.

- Learner rearranges word parts. Wait for responses.

Say to the Learner,

"Say 'cowboy'."   "Say it again but don't say 'cow'."

"Say 'hotdog'."   "Say it again, but don't say 'dog'."

"Say 'airplane'."   "Say it again, but don't say 'air'."

Continue this activity using the following words and other words listed under PreReading Level 4,
① COMBINE WORDS and ② DIVIDE WORDS.

popcorn	airport	haystack
classmate	pancake	rainbow
bathtub	moonlight	sunshine

When the Learner is comfortable with this activity, try this variation,

"Say 'sport'."   "Say it again, but don't say /s/."

"Say 'track'."   "Say it again, but don't say /t/."

"Say 'brain'."   "Say it again, but don't say /b/."

Continue this activity using the following words.

t/an	b/all	n/ear	s/tyle	d/art
s/at	t/ar	t/each	p/lump	h/and
r/ace	f/old	r/ate	m/arch	p/age
b/oil	r/ink	t/ape	s/ample	b/end
b/lind	c/laim	v/alley	n/eat	s/lice
s/mile	h/itch	s/lime	s/well	f/lame

Continue to review the activities in PreReading Levels 1 through 4 as you move on to PreReading Level 5.

SONDAY SYSTEM 1 LEARNING PLAN

PreReading Level 4• Can We Move On?

CAN WE MOVE ON?

Before continuing on to PreReading Level 5, the student should be able to comfortably do the following:

- Recite the alphabet with 100% accuracy.
- Point to randomly named letters on the Alphabet Strip
- Clap patterns involving 4 claps
- Name 3 words beginning with each of 6 different dictated consonant sounds
- Name 4-5 rhyming words that match the pattern of 6 different given words
- Print 21 upper case letters (on elementary lined paper for kindergarten or first graders; on secondary paper for older students)
- Print 21 lower case letters (first grade and older)
- Combine compound words with 100% accuracy, with and without music
- Divide compound words with 100% accuracy, with and without music
- Combine word parts, closure, with 100% accuracy
- Combine sounds, closure, with 100% accuracy
- Rearrange words with 90% accuracy
- Delete the first sound of a given word with 90% accuracy

Continue to practice the alphabet, clapping, onset sound, rhyme, printing, combining words and word parts, segmenting words and word parts when introducing new material in Level 5.

PreReading Level 5 • Converting Letter to Sound

Letters are symbols for sounds. Each sound is represented by a letter or group of letters.
By learning the alphabetic code, one can unlock the door to reading and spelling.

MATERIALS NEEDED

- Watch Instructional Video • Alphabet Strips (upper and lower case letters) • Letter Tactile Cards • Sound Cards 1-17 • Sand Tray
- Audio Pronunciation CD

REVIEW

As new activities are introduced in PreReading Level 5, continue to:
- Sing and Say the Alphabet
- Play with Beginning Sounds
- Combine Words
- Name the Letters in Sequence
- Play with Rhyming Words
- Divide Words
- Seek and Find letters
- Trace Letters
- Combine Word Parts
- Play with Rhythm
- Print Letters
- Combine Sounds
- Rearrange Words

CHECK FOR KNOWLEDGE

Find the white Sound Cards which have letters on one side, a key word and picture on the reverse. The cards are numbered in the order in which they will be taught. Using Sound Cards 1-17,

- Learner <u>reads</u> the letters on each card and says the sound aloud. Place the known cards in a pile and return the unknown cards to the Sound Card pack.
- Dictate consonant sounds from the "known" pile, one at a time.
- Learner spells by printing the letter representing the sound on paper or in sand.
- Place the cards that the Learner can spell in Pile 1.
  Place the cards that the Learner can not spell in Pile 2.
  Pile 1 will be reviewed under ① READ SOUNDS
  Pile 2 will be learned under ③ INTRODUCE NEW MATERIAL.

LESSON PLAN STRUCTURE

At this PreReading Level the Learning Plan begins to follow a structure that will be used for the rest of the Sonday System 1. The parts introduced here are:

① READ SOUNDS   ② SPELL SOUNDS   ③ INTRODUCE NEW MATERIAL

SONDAY SYSTEM 1 LEARNING PLAN

PreReading Level 5 ● Converting Letter to Sound

 ## READ SOUNDS (visual)

- Review Sound Cards, Pile 1, at every Session.
- Learner reads the sound of each card aloud.

 ## SPELL SOUNDS (visual/auditory/tactile)

- Dictate each sound from Pile 1 at every Session.
- Learner repeats the sound.
- Learner writes the letter in sand or on paper.

 ## INTRODUCE NEW MATERIAL (visual/auditory/tactile)

Teach one new sound from Pile 2 at each Session. Sounds that could be read but <u>not</u> spelled are in Pile 2. Correct sounds are modeled on the video. Encourage the Learner to use clean, clipped sounds.

- Show the Learner a Sound Card.
- Say the sound and give the key word which is found on the back of the Sound Card.
- Learner repeats the sound and traces it on the table with two fingers of the writing hand 5 times while repeating the sound. (Learner may also trace on the floor, in a sand tray, on a carpet sample or chalkboard, with finger paint or shaving cream, etc.)
- Learner writes the sound on paper 5 times while saying the sound aloud.
- Place the card in Pile 1 for review at the next Session.

HELPERS NOTE	If the most recent sound taught cannot be recalled in the next Session, teach it again.

After teaching all sounds in Pile 2, teach the remaining cards until Sound Cards 1–17 have been learned.

PreReading Level 5 • Converting Letter to Sound

4 READING GAME (visual/auditory/kinesthetic)

- Using the Alphabet Strip, Learner names the letters of the alphabet and gives the sounds of the letters that have been taught, pointing to each letter.
- Fold the Alphabet Strip so that only <u>a</u> through <u>g</u> are exposed. Ask,

  "Find the letter that says /d/." (Use the sound, not the name.)

  "Good! What is the name of that letter?"

  "Now point to the letter before the /d/. What is the name of that letter?" (Ask for the sound of c if it has been learned.)

  "Now point to the letter after the /d/. What is the name of that letter?" (Vowel sounds will be taught later.)

- Repeat this dialogue until your Learner can easily identify all of the letters, name the letters before and after the target letter and give the sounds for the letters <u>b</u>, <u>d</u> and <u>f</u>.
- Add the next segment of the Alphabet Strip so the letters <u>a</u> through <u>n</u> are exposed.
- Repeat the same routine but select random letters from <u>a</u> through <u>n</u> and add the sounds for <u>j</u>, <u>k</u>, <u>l</u>, <u>m</u>, and <u>n</u>. (Use letter names for all letters where the sound has not been taught.)
- Expose the <u>o</u> through <u>s</u> segment, then the <u>t</u> through <u>z</u> segment when previous segments have been mastered.

Continue to review the activities in PreReading Levels 1 through 5 as you move on to the Reading Levels.

CAN WE MOVE ON?

Before continuing on to Reading, Level 1, the student should be able to comfortably do the following:

- Recite the alphabet with 100% accuracy.
- Point to randomly named letters on the Alphabet Strip
- Clap patterns involving 6 claps
- Name 3 words beginning with each of 8 different dictated consonant sounds
- Name 5 rhyming words that match the pattern of 8 different given words
- Print 23 upper case letters (on elementary lined paper for kindergarten or first graders; on secondary paper for older students)
- Print 23 lower case letters (first grade and older)
- Combine and divide compound words with 100% accuracy, with and without music
- Combine sounds, closure, with 100% accuracy
- Rearrange words with 90% accuracy
- Recite the sounds of 17 consonants using the Sound Cards
- Write 17 consonant sounds from dictation

Move on the Reading Level 1.

Reading Level 1

MATERIALS NEEDED

- Watch Instructional Video • Sound Cards 1-18 • Sand Tray • Paper and pencil • Nerf Ball • Book to read

1 READ SOUNDS

 2 MIN.

- Review Sound Cards **1-17**
- Learner reads sound of each card aloud.
- Go through the cards rapidly. The goal is to have automatic responses.

® Do this at the beginning of every Session. Reading individual letters quickly is necessary before reading words.

REMINDER	Ask for clean, clipped consonant sounds. Watch Video or Audio Pronunciation CD for correct modeling of sounds.

2 SPELL SOUNDS

 2 MIN.

- Dictate the following sounds, one at a time.

    b   m   s   p   t   l   f   d   n   r

- Learner repeats the sound.
- Learner writes the letter on paper or in the sand tray.

QUESTIONS TO ASK THE LEARNER	No questions this level.

BALL TOSS GAME	• Say a word while you toss or roll a Nerf Ball to the Learner.
	  Learner returns it while repeating just the beginning sound of the word.
	    Example: Throw the ball and say "sat"
	    Learner returns it and says, "sat, /s/"
	• For a list of words, see Word Book, page 1.

SONDAY SYSTEM 1 LEARNING PLAN
Reading Level 1

③ INTRODUCE NEW MATERIAL

1. Introduce New Sound
• Show the Card and say the sound to the Learner.
• Learner repeats the sound and traces it in the sand tray, on the table or on paper.

Card: **Sound Card 18** | a | /a/ as in apple

Rule: Short <u>a</u> is found at the beginning or middle of a word.
• Use Sound Cards to form <u>at</u> words. Follow video instructions.

• Place the <u>a</u> Sound Card on the table facing the Learner, then place the <u>t</u> Sound Card after it.

| a | | t |

• Sound out the <u>a</u> and <u>t</u> and blend the two sounds into the word <u>at</u>.
• Learner traces <u>a</u> and <u>t</u> while saying the sounds out loud. Then have the Learner say the word.
• Do this four times.

• Put the <u>m</u> Sound Card before the <u>a</u> on the table.

| m | | a | | t |

• Learner sounds out the three letters and puts them together to make a word.
• Learner traces the word in the sand tray while sounding it out.
• Learner reads the word just written.

• Learner reads words from the Word Book, page 1, column 1.

• Dictate the following words.
• Learner repeats each word, <u>Touch Spells</u> each word and says each sound out loud while writing the word on paper.

     sat   bat   cat   mat   fat   pat   rat
• Learner reads the list of words just written.

2. Review New Sound
Use Sound Cards to form <u>an</u> words. Follow routine above.
• Learner reads words from the Word Book, page 1, column 2.

• Dictate the following words.
• Learner repeats each word, <u>Touch Spells</u> each word and says each sound out loud while writing the word on paper.

     pan   ran   can   man   fan   tan
• Learner reads the list of words just written.

CORRECTING SPELLING ERRORS

• Use questions to help Learner self correct when spelling errors are made.
    If <u>pan</u> is spelled as <u>pna</u>, say,
        "<u>Touch Spell</u> the word."
        "Now rewrite the sounds in order."
• Learner rewrites the misspelled word so it is correctly spelled twice.

Reading Level 1

4 READ ALOUD

10 MIN.

- Choose one of the following activities at each session.

a) Word Book, page 1. Learner reads words aloud.

b) Read a book. If your Learner can read a book, do it now. If your Learner cannot read a book, read to the Learner. See page 128 of the Word Book for a list of beginning reading books.

HELPER'S NOTE

Continue using Sound Cards to form words in the next Levels so the Learner can manipulate sounds and see words form.

Reading Level 2

MATERIALS NEEDED

• Watch Instructional Video • Sound Cards 1–18 • Sand Tray • Paper and pencil • Nerf Ball • Book to read

① READ SOUNDS

• Review Sound Cards **1–18**
• Learner reads sound of each card aloud.
• Go through the cards rapidly. The goal is to have automatic responses.

® Do this at the beginning of every Session. Reading individual letters quickly is necessary before reading words.

REMINDER | Mix the Sound Cards so the Learner cannot memorize the sequence.

② SPELL SOUNDS

• Dictate the following sounds, one at a time.

s a j b r h v t f

• Learner repeats the sound.
• Learner writes the letter on paper or in the sand tray.

QUESTIONS TO ASK THE LEARNER | Write two ways to spell /k/. (Answer: c, k)

| | **REMINDER** | Give the sound when a slash appears on both sides of a letter. Example: /k/ |

BALL TOSS GAME

• Say a word while you toss or roll a Nerf Ball to the Learner.
  Learner returns it while repeating just the beginning sound of the word.
    Example: Throw the ball and say "bat"
    Learner returns it and says, "bat, /b/"
• For a list of words, see Word Book, page 1.

SONDAY SYSTEM 1 LEARNING PLAN

Reading Level 2

 ## READ WORDS

 5 MIN.

Learner reads aloud from the following sources:

1. Word Book, page 1, column 1, <u>at</u> words.
2. Word Book, page 1, column 2, <u>an</u> words.
3. Word Book, page 1, column 3, mixed words.

REMINDER | Have the Learner use the Reading Marker or a pointer finger when reading words.

 ## SPELL WORDS

 7 MIN.

- Dictate the following words to the Learner.
- Learner repeats each word, <u>Touch Spells</u> each word and says each sound out loud while writing the word on paper.
- Dictate each word aloud, reading down the columns.
- ® Column at the far left below indicates which sound is being practiced in each row of words.
- ® Dictate words for seven minutes, correcting errors when they occur. Material is provided for additional Sessions.

<u>at</u>	at	sat	cat	hat
<u>a</u>		_____	_____	_____
<u>an</u>	an	ran	pan	fan
<u>at</u>	rat	pat	mat	bat
<u>an</u>	man	tan	can	van
<u>a</u>		_____	_____	_____

- Learner reads the list of words just written.

5 INTRODUCE NEW MATERIAL

5 MIN.

1. Introduce New Sound
- Show the Card and say the sound.
- Learner repeats the sound and traces it in the sand tray, or on the table.

Card: **Sound Card 18**

 a   /a/ as in apple

Rule: Short <u>a</u> is found at the beginning or middle of a word.

- Use Sound Cards to form words in Word Book, page 2. Follow Instructional Video.

- Learner reads words from the Word Book, page 2.

- Dictate the following words.
- Learner repeats each word, <u>Touch Spells</u> each word and says each sound out loud while writing the word on paper.

map   sad   tap   had   gag   cab

- Learner reads the list of words just written.
- ® After teaching the sound, enter some of the words above in the blank spaces of ④ **SPELL WORDS.**

CORRECTING SPELLING ERRORS	• Use questions to help Learner self correct when spelling errors are made. When <u>map</u> is spelled as <u>nap</u>, say, "Touch Spell that word." Wiggle the /m/ finger. "What is the sound on this finger? How do you write it?" • Learner rewrites the misspelled word so it is correctly spelled twice.

6 READ ALOUD

10 MIN.

- Choose one of the following activities at each Session.

a) Word Book, page 2. Learner reads words aloud.

b) Read a book. If your Learner can read a book, do it now. If your Learner cannot read a book, read to the Learner. See page 128 of the Word Book for a list of beginning reading books.

HELPER'S NOTE	Reinforcement of previously taught material is the key to cementing information into long term memory. Reading and spelling are for the long term.

Reading Level 3

MATERIALS NEEDED

- Watch Instructional Video • Sound Cards 1–19 • Sand Tray • Paper and pencil • Nerf Ball
- Word Cards (pink) • Word Book • Reading Marker • Board Game • Book to read

---

1 READ SOUNDS

2 MIN.

- Review Sound Cards **1–18**
- Learner reads sound of each card aloud.
- Go through the cards rapidly. The goal is to have automatic responses.

® Do this at the beginning of every Session. Reading individual letters quickly is necessary before reading words.

REMINDER	Ask for two sounds of <u>a</u>, short and long. The long sound is the same as the name of the letter.

---

2 SPELL SOUNDS

2 MIN.

- Dictate the following sounds, one at a time.

p r a b n g h l d

- Learner repeats the sound.
- Learner writes the letter on paper or in the sand tray.

QUESTIONS TO ASK THE LEARNER	Write two ways to spell /k/. (Answer: c, k)	
	REMINDER	Give the sound when slashes appear on both sides of a letter. Example: /k/

BALL TOSS GAME	• Say a word while you toss or roll a Nerf Ball to the Learner.
	   Learner returns it while repeating just the beginning sound of the word.
	      Example: Throw the ball and say "man"
	     Learner returns it and says, "/m/"
	• For a list of words, see Word Book, page 2.	

SONDAY SYSTEM 1 LEARNING PLAN
Reading Level 3

 3 ## READ WORDS 5 MIN.

Learner reads aloud from the following sources. Material is provided for several Sessions.

1. Word Book, page 1, column 3, mixed words.
2. Word Cards, Short a (pink).
3. Word Book, page 2, Short a.
4. Word Book, page 3, Review Short a.
5. Word Book, page 130, Fluency practice, Level 3.

REMINDER | Have the Learner use the Reading Marker or a pointer finger when reading words.

 4 ## SPELL WORDS 7 MIN.

- Dictate the following words to the Learner.
- Learner repeats each word, <u>Touch Spells</u> each word and says each sound out loud while writing the word on paper.
- Dictate each word aloud, reading down the columns.
- ® Column at the far left below indicates which sound is being practiced in each row of words.
- ® Dictate words for seven minutes, correcting errors when they occur. Material is provided for additional Sessions.

<u>a</u>	sad	mad	had	fat
<u>a</u>	pat	cat	bat	pan
<u>i</u>				
<u>a</u>	fan	ran	tag	lap
<u>a</u>	sat	bad	cap	bag
<u>i</u>				

- Learner reads the list of words just written.

5

INTRODUCE NEW MATERIAL

1. Introduce New Sound
- Show the Card and say the sound.
- Learner repeats the sound and traces it in the sand tray, on the table or on paper.

Card: **Sound Card 19** /i/ as in itch

Rule: Short i is found at the beginning or middle of a word.
- Use Sound Cards to form it, in words, Word Book, page 4.

- Learner reads corresponding words from the Word Book, page 4.

- Dictate the following words.
- Learner repeats each word, Touch Spells each word and says each sound out loud while writing the word on paper.

| pit | sit | hit | bit | • | pin | tin | fin | sin |

- Learner reads the list of words just written.

® After teaching the sound, enter some of the words above in the blank spaces of ④ **SPELL WORDS.**

CORRECTING SPELLING ERRORS

- Use questions to help Learner self correct when spelling errors are made.
  When pit is spelled as pat, say,
      "Touch Spell that word." Wiggle the vowel finger.
      "What is the sound on this finger? How do you write it?"
- Learner rewrites the misspelled word so it is correctly spelled twice.

---

2. Review New Sound
- Show the Card and say the sound.
- Learner repeats the sound and traces it in the sand tray.

Card: **Sound Card 19** /i/ as in itch

Use Sound Cards to form words using all known consonants. Follow video instructions.

- Learner reads words from the Word Book, page 4, columns 2 and 3.

- Dictate the following words.
- Learner repeats each word, Touch Spells each word and says each sound out loud while writing the word on paper.

| lip | rim | hid | sip | dig | dim | rig |

® After teaching the sound, enter some of the words above in the blank spaces of ④ **SPELL WORDS.**

SONDAY SYSTEM 1 LEARNING PLAN

Reading Level 3

6 READ ALOUD

- Choose one of the following activities at each Session.

a) Word Book, page 3.

b) Board Game, Word Cards (pink).

c) Read a book. If your Learner can read a book, do it now. If your Learner cannot read a book, read to the Learner. See page 128 of the Word Book for a list of beginning reading books.

HELPER'S NOTE	Use as many Sessions as you need to complete this Level. Begin each Session by repeating: ① READ SOUNDS ② SPELL SOUNDS ③ READ WORDS ④ SPELL WORDS
CHECK FOR MASTERY	Use Mastery Check 3 on the following page to check progress.

Mastery Check for Reading
Use after Level 3

Using the Sonday System 1 Learning Plan format, incorporate Mastery Check for Reading in the 3. Read Words section. Have the Learner read the words aloud. Time limit is 30 seconds. If fewer than 90% of the words are read accurately, teach two more sessions and give Form B during the 3. Read Words section of the third session. Alternate Forms A and B at every third session until the Learner reaches 90%.

HELPER'S NOTE	Both Form A and B contain the same words but in a different order to avoid memorization of the sequence and require the Learner to read each word.

Have the student read the test from the Word Book, p. 138.

Reading Level 3 – Form A			
bit	in	fit	fin
tin	lip	pin	rig
rim	bag	him	tan
pad	bid	nap	zip
sit	did	pit	pig

Reading Level 3 – Form B			
pad	bid	fin	fit
sit	pin	rig	did
tan	him	in	bit
lip	tin	zip	nap
pig	pit	bag	rim

Count the number of words correctly read and multiply by 5 to obtain the percentage correct or use the Conversion Chart below.

CONVERSION CHART

# Correct	%	# Correct	%	# Correct	%
1	5%	8	40%	15	75%
2	10%	9	45%	16	80%
3	15%	10	50%	17	85%
4	20%	11	55%	18	90%
5	25%	12	60%	19	95%
6	30%	13	65%	20	100%
7	35%	14	70%		

The Learner should have 90% accuracy on the this test and 85% accuracy on the Spelling Mastery Check before moving to the next level.

Mastery Check for Spelling
Use after Level 3

Dictate the following words, reading down the columns. Repeat the words if necessary, but don't help the Learner make corrections. The goal is to determine what has been learned and how well the Learner can spell independently.

sat	map	bag	van
fit	him	lid	zip
jam	cap	ran	sad
big	sit	hip	rig
can	rib	fan	hid

If 17 of the 20 words have been correctly spelled proceed to the next Level.

If four or more words are misspelled categorize the errors in the columns below by marking the letter or letters which represent the correct spelling. For example:

If	sat	is spelled as	sap	mark t
If	lid	is spelled as	lib	mark d
If	jam	is spelled as	jim	mark a
If	can	is spelled as	cam	mark n

Errors	Word Book page	Errors	Word Book page	Errors	Word Book page
b ☐	122	j ☐	122	s ☐	123
c ☐	122	l ☐	122	t ☐	123
d ☐	122	m ☐	122	v ☐	123
f ☐	122	n ☐	123	z ☐	123
g ☐	122	p ☐	123	a ☐	2, 3
h ☐	122	r ☐	123	i ☐	4

When you have identified the letters/sounds that need more practice, you may return to Levels 1–3 for four more Sessions. The Word Book pages listed above will provide lists of words to use in creating learning plans. After at least four practice Sessions give this test again before moving to Level 4.

Reading Level 4

MATERIALS NEEDED

• Watch Instructional Video • Sound Cards 1–20 • Sand Tray • Paper and pencil • Nerf Ball
• Word Cards (pink, blue) • Word Book • Reading Marker • Reading Window and Strip 4 • Board Game • Book to read

---

1 ## READ SOUNDS 2 MIN.

• Review Sound Cards **1–19**
• Learner reads sound of each card aloud.
• Go through the cards rapidly. The goal is to have automatic responses.

® Do this at the beginning of every Session. Reading individual letters quickly is necessary before reading words.

| REMINDER | Ask for two sounds of <u>a</u> and <u>i</u>, short and long. The long sound is the same as the name of the letter. |

---

2 ## SPELL SOUNDS 2 MIN.

• Dictate the following sounds, one at a time. Dictate short sounds of the vowels.

d   a   m   v   i   g   p   n   r   f

• Learner repeats the sound.
• Learner writes the letter on paper or in the sand tray.

QUESTIONS TO ASK THE LEARNER	No questions this Level.
BALL TOSS GAME	• Say a word while you toss or roll a Nerf Ball to the Learner. Learner returns it while repeating just the beginning sound of the word. Example: Throw the ball and say "fan" Learner returns it and says, "/f/" • For a list of words, see Word Book, page 3.

SONDAY SYSTEM 1 LEARNING PLAN

Reading Level 4

---

3 READ WORDS

 5 MIN.

Learner reads aloud from the following sources. Material is provided for several Sessions.

1. Word Book, page 3, Review Short a.
2. Word Book, page 4, Short i.
3. Word Cards, Short a and i (pink and blue, mixed).
4. Word Book, review any previous pages.

4 SPELL WORDS

 7 MIN.

- Dictate the following words to the Learner.
- Learner repeats each word, <u>Touch Spells</u> each word and says each sound out loud while writing the word on paper.
- Dictate each word aloud, reading down the columns.
- ® Column at the far left below indicates which sound is being practiced in each row of words.
- ® Dictate words for seven minutes, correcting errors when they occur. Material is provided for additional Sessions.

<u>i</u>	fit	sip	pig	pit
<u>a</u>	can	rag	lap	sad
<u>o</u>				
<u>i</u>	jig	lid	bin	hid
<u>a</u>	mad	map	hat	tap
<u>o</u>				

- Learner reads the list of words just written.

- At each Session, dictate two of the following phrases.
- Learner repeats each phrase and writes it on paper.

sad man	bad hat
bit him	big pit
tin man	mad pig

- Learner reads aloud the phrases just written.

INTRODUCE NEW MATERIAL

5 MIN.

1. Introduce New Sound
• Show the Card and say the sound.
• Learner repeats the sound and traces it in the sand tray.

Card: **Sound Card 20** o /o/ as in octopus

Rule: Short <u>o</u> is found at the beginning or middle of a word.

• Learner reads words from the Word Book, page 5.

• Dictate the following words.
• Learner repeats each word, <u>Touch Spells</u> each word and says each sound out loud while writing the word on paper.

| mop | dot | on | hot | pop | log |

• Learner reads the list of words just written.
® After teaching the sound, enter some of the words above in the blank spaces of ④ **SPELL WORDS.**

CORRECTING SPELLING ERRORS

• Use questions to help Learner self correct when spelling errors are made.
  When <u>dot</u> is spelled as <u>bot</u>, say,
      "Hands up! What's the first sound in 'dot'?"
      "Which hand shows that sound? Trace it and say /d/."
• Learner rewrites the misspelled word so it is correctly spelled twice. Watch video for b-d demonstration.

READ ALOUD

10 MIN.

• Choose one of the following activities at each Session.

a) Reading Strip 4.

b) Sentences and Phrases, Word Book, page 6.

c) Board Game, Word Cards (pink and blue, mixed).

d) Read a book. If your Learner can read a book, do it now. If your Learner cannot read a book, read to the Learner.
   See page 128 of the Word Book for a list of beginning reading books.

HELPER'S NOTE

Good job! Now you have three vowels and the number of words that you can read is growing.

Reading Level 5

MATERIALS NEEDED

- Watch Instructional Video • Sound Cards 1–21 • Sand Tray • Paper and pencil • Nerf Ball • Word Cards (pink, blue, green)
- Sight Word Cards (red) 1–2 • Word Book • Reading Marker • Reading Window and Strips 4–5 • Board Game • Book to read

---

1 READ SOUNDS 2 MIN.

- Review Sound Cards **1–20**
- Learner reads sound of each card aloud.
- Go through the cards rapidly. The goal is to have automatic responses.

® Do this at the beginning of every Session. Reading individual letters quickly is necessary before reading words.

REMINDER	Ask for two sounds of <u>a</u>, <u>i</u> and <u>o</u>, short and long. The long sound is the same as the name of the letter.

---

2 SPELL SOUNDS 2 MIN.

- Dictate the following sounds, one at a time. Dictate short sounds of the vowels.

  t s a h i j l o n

- Learner repeats the sound.
- Learner writes the letter on paper or in the sand tray.

QUESTIONS TO ASK THE LEARNER	What are two ways to write /k/? (Answer: c, k)	
	REMINDER	Give the sound when a slash appears on both sides of a letter. Example: /k/

BALL TOSS GAME	• Say a word while you toss or roll a Nerf Ball to the Learner.
	   Learner returns it while repeating just the beginning sound of the word.
	      Example: Throw the ball and say "lid"
	      Learner returns it and says, "/l/"
	• For a list of words, see Word Book, page 3.	

SONDAY SYSTEM 1 LEARNING PLAN

Reading Level 5

---

③ READ WORDS 5 MIN.

Learner reads aloud from the following sources. Material is provided for several Sessions.

1. Word Cards, Short o (green).
2. Word Cards, Short a and i (pink and blue, mixed).
3. Word Book, p. 5. Short o.
4. Word Book, p. 4. Short i.
5. Word Book, review any previous pages.

REMINDER Learner may use Reading Marker when reading the Word Book.

④ SPELL WORDS 7 MIN.

- Dictate the following words to the Learner.
- Learner repeats each word, <u>Touch Spells</u> each word and says each sound out loud while writing the word on paper.
- Dictate each word aloud, reading down the columns.
- ® Column at the far left below indicates which sound is being practiced in each row of words.
- ® Dictate words for seven minutes, correcting errors when they occur. Material is provided for additional Sessions.

<u>o</u>	cot	lot	mop	pop
<u>a</u>	man	pat	ran	tap
<u>o</u>	hop	dot	top	log
<u>i</u>	pin	big	bit	lip
<u>x</u>		___	___	___
<u>sight</u>		___	___	___

- Learner reads the list of words just written.

- At each Session, dictate two of the following phrases.
- Learner repeats the phrase and writes it on paper.

big job	top hat
hot dog	tip it
tin can	fat cat

- Learner reads aloud the phrases just written.

Reading Level 5

 5

INTRODUCE NEW MATERIAL

 5 MIN.

1. Introduce New Sight Words
• Teach the following Sight Words, one in each Session.
• These words cannot be sounded out and need to be memorized.

Card: **Sight Word Cards 1-2** | a | the |

• Show the Learner one Sight Word Card, say it aloud and ask the Learner to repeat it.
• Learner traces the letters on the table, or in the sand tray while saying the letter names.
• Learner repeats the word before and after tracing.
• Learner writes new Sight Word on paper.
® After teaching, enter these words in the blank spaces of ④ **SPELL WORDS,** to dictate during the next Session.

2. Introduce New Sound
• Show the Card and say the sound.
• Learner repeats the sound and traces it in the sand tray.

Card: **Sound Card 21** | x | /ks/ as in fox

• Learner reads words from the Word Book, page 7.

• Dictate the following words.
• Learner repeats each word, <u>Touch Spells</u> each word and says each sound out loud while writing the word on paper.

| | | | | | |
| mix | tax | fox | box | ax | fix |

• Learner reads the list of words just written.
® After teaching the sound, enter some of the words above in the blank spaces of ④ **SPELL WORDS.**

CORRECTING SPELLING ERRORS

• Use questions to help Learner self correct when spelling errors are made.
  When <u>fix</u> is spelled as <u>fiks</u> or <u>fics</u>, ask,
      "What is the last sound in that word?"
      "What is another way of spelling /ks/?"
• Learner rewrites the misspelled word so it is correctly spelled twice.

SONDAY SYSTEM 1 LEARNING PLAN

Reading Level 5

6 READ ALOUD

10 MIN.

- Choose one of the following activities at each Session.

a) Reading Strip 5.

b) Sentences, Word Book, page 8.

c) Reread Reading Strips 4.

d) Read a book. If the Learner can read a book, do it now. If the Learner cannot read a book, read to the Learner. See page 128 of the Word Book for a list of beginning reading books.

e) Board Game. Word Cards (pink, blue, and green, mixed).

| HELPER'S NOTE | Are the words with short <u>a</u> becoming easier to read? Good job! |

Reading Level 6

MATERIALS NEEDED

- Watch Instructional Video • Sound Cards 1-22 • Sand Tray • Paper and pencil • Nerf Ball • Word Cards (pink, blue, green)
- Sight Word Cards (red) 1-5 • Word Book • Reading Marker • Reading Window and Strips 4-6 • Board Game • Book to read

1 READ SOUNDS

2 MIN.

- Review Sound Cards **1–21**
- Learner reads sound of each card aloud.
- Go through the cards rapidly. The goal is to have automatic responses.

® Do this at the beginning of every Session.

| REMINDER | Ask for two sounds of <u>a</u>, <u>i</u> and <u>o</u>, short and long. The long sound is the same as the name of the letter. |

2 SPELL SOUNDS

2 MIN.

- Dictate the following sounds, one at a time. Dictate short vowel sounds.

  o f x a b s m d i h

- Learner repeats the sound.
- Learner writes the letter on paper or in the sand tray.

QUESTIONS TO ASK THE LEARNER	No questions this level.
BALL TOSS GAME	• Say a word while you toss or roll a Nerf Ball to the Learner. Learner returns it while repeating just the ending sound of the word. Example: Throw the ball and say "pass" Learner returns it and says, "pass, /s/" • For a list of words, see Word Book, page 3.

SONDAY SYSTEM 1 LEARNING PLAN

Reading Level 6

3 READ WORDS

5 MIN.

Learner reads aloud from the following sources. Material is provided for several Sessions.

1. Word Cards, short a, i and o (pink, blue and green, mixed).
2. Word Book, page 9, Review a, i, o, x.
3. Sight Word Cards 1–2.
4. Word Book, page 130, Fluency practice, Level 6.
5. Word Book, review any previous pages.

REMINDER If the Learner does not readily recognize the word, have the Learner trace the letters on the table and say each sound aloud, then blend the sounds into a word.

4 SPELL WORDS

7 MIN.

- Dictate the following words to the Learner.
- Learner repeats each word, <u>Touch Spells</u> each word and says each sound out loud while writing the word on paper.
- Dictate each word aloud, reading down the columns.
- ® Column at the far left below indicates which sound is being practiced in each row of words.
- ® Dictate words for seven minutes, correcting errors when they occur. Material is provided for additional Sessions.

<u>x</u>	fox	six	box	tax
<u>a</u>	had	ran	pat	bat
<u>i</u>	pit	dim	hip	sit
<u>o</u>	hop	rob	got	mob
<u>ay</u>		___	___	___
<u>sight</u>	a	the	___	___

- Learner reads the list of words just written.

- At each Session, dictate two of the following phrases or sentences.
- Learner repeats the phrase or sentence and writes it on paper.

I got the job.	Pat the dog.
The fox hid.	Tap the pan.
Sip the pop.	Dig a pit.

- Learner reads aloud the phrases just written.

Reading Level 6

5 — ## INTRODUCE NEW MATERIAL

1. Introduce New Sight Words
- Teach the following Sight Words, one in each Session.
- These words cannot be sounded out and need to be memorized.

Card: **Sight Word Cards 3-5** | to | do | is |

- Show the Learner one Sight Word Card, say it aloud and ask the Learner to repeat it.
- Learner traces the letters on the table while saying the letter names.
- Learner repeats the word before and after tracing.
- Learner writes new Sight Word on paper.

® After teaching, enter these words in the blank spaces of ④ **SPELL WORDS,** to dictate during the next Session.

2. Introduce New Sound
- Show the Card and say the sound.
- Learner repeats the sound and traces it in the sand tray.

Card: **Sound Card 22** | ay | long /a/ as in day

Rule: <u>ay</u> is always used at the end of a word.

- Learner reads words from the Word Book, page 10.

- Dictate the following words.
- Learner repeats each word, <u>Touch Spells</u> each word and says each sound out loud while writing the word on paper.

   may   ray   say   pay   day   lay

- Learner reads the list of words just written.

® After teaching the sound, enter some of the words above in the blank spaces of ④ **SPELL WORDS.**

CORRECTING SPELLING ERRORS

- Use questions to help Learner self correct when spelling errors are made.
  When <u>pay</u> is spelled as <u>pae</u> or <u>pa</u>, ask,
     "What is the last sound in that word?"
     "How do you write that sound at the end of a word?"
- Learner rewrites the misspelled word so it is correctly spelled twice.

SONDAY SYSTEM 1 LEARNING PLAN

Reading Level 6

READ ALOUD

10 MIN.

• Choose one of the following activities at each Session.

a) Reading Strip 6.

b) Sentences, Word Book, page 11.

c) Read a book.
 - Sonday Readers, 6a, 6b, 6c.
 - See page 128 of the Word Book for a list of beginning reading books.

d) Reread Reading Strips 4–5.

e) Board Game. Word Cards (pink, blue and green mixed).

HELPER'S NOTE	Take as many Sessions as you need to finish Level 6. Each time you start a learning Session, repeat ①, ②, ③ and ④. We are working for fluency and the automatic response. Move ahead when your Learner is very comfortable at this Level.
CHECK FOR MASTERY	Use Mastery Check 6, on the following page, to check progress.

Mastery Check for Reading
Use after Level 6

Using the Sonday System 1 Learning Plan format, incorporate Mastery Check for Reading in the 3. Read Words section. Have the Learner read the words aloud. Time limit is 30 seconds. If fewer than 90% of the words are read accurately, teach two more sessions and give Form B during the 3. Read Words section of the third session. Alternate Forms A and B at every third session until the Learner reaches 90%.

HELPER'S NOTE	Both Form A and B contain the same words but in a different order to avoid memorization of the sequence and require the Learner to read each word.

Have the student read the test from the Word Book, p. 139.

Reading Level 6 – Form A

jab	ray	gag	day
say	sap	pay	tag
max	jog	fix	on
if	fill	it	bill
boss	cob	not	off

Reading Level 6 – Form B

off	nod	fill	if
cob	boss	gag	day
jab	ray	pay	tag
say	on	fix	sap
it	bill	max	jog

Count the number of words correctly read and multiply by 5 to obtain the percentage correct or use the Conversion Chart below.

CONVERSION CHART

# Correct	%	# Correct	%	# Correct	%
1	5%	8	40%	15	75%
2	10%	9	45%	16	80%
3	15%	10	50%	17	85%
4	20%	11	55%	18	90%
5	25%	12	60%	19	95%
6	30%	13	65%	20	100%
7	35%	14	70%		

The Learner should have 90% accuracy on the this test and 85% accuracy on the Spelling Mastery Check before moving to the next level.

Mastery Check for Spelling
Use after Level 6

Dictate the following words, reading down the columns. Repeat the words if necessary, but don't help the Learner make corrections. The goal is to determine what has been learned and how well the Learner can spell independently.

rat	rap	jam	hay
hit	mad	mop	rod
fog	fix	lap	lip
pin	bay	say	ray
box	vat	rig	hot

If 17 of the 20 words have been correctly spelled proceed to the next Level.

If four or more words are misspelled categorize the errors in the columns below by marking the letter or letters which represent the correct spelling. For example:

If	vat	is spelled as	fat	mark v
If	mop	is spelled as	map	mark o
If	bay	is spelled as	ba	mark ay
If	lid	is spelled as	led	mark i

Errors	Word Book page	Errors	Word Book page	Errors	Word Book page
b ☐	124	l ☐	124	v ☐	125
c ☐	124	m ☐	125	x ☐	7
d ☐	124	n ☐	125	z ☐	125
f ☐	124	p ☐	125	a ☐	2, 3
g ☐	124	r ☐	125	i ☐	4
h ☐	124	s ☐	125	o ☐	5
j ☐	124	t ☐	125	ay ☐	10

When you have identified the letters/sounds that need more practice you may return to Levels 4–6 for four more Sessions or you may create Personalized Learning Plans following the instructions on the next two pages. The Word Book pages listed above will provide lists of words to use in creating learning plans. After at least four practice Sessions give this test again before moving to Level 7.

Using the form on the following page, construct a Personal Learning Plan to practice words and sounds that were missed in the Mastery Check along with words that have been mastered.

READ SOUNDS

- Use Sound Cards.
- Review all sounds that have been taught. Do this at every Session.

SPELL SOUNDS

- Use known sounds. Include those missed in the Mastery Check.
- Dictate 10 review sounds in 2 minutes or less at every Session.

READ WORDS

- Use Word Cards or Word Book lists that have been introduced.
- Read review words for 5 minutes at every Session.

SPELL WORDS

- Use words from the Word Cards or the Word Book that have been practiced. Include words that reinforce the sounds spelled incorrectly on the Mastery Check.
- Use sentences from the Word Book or create your own using words and sounds that have been taught.

READ ALOUD

- Use a Book to read, Reading Strips, or Board Game.

Learning Plan

1 READ SOUNDS 2 MIN.

- Review Sound Cards _____

2 SPELL SOUNDS 2 MIN.

___ ___ ___ ___ ___ ___ ___ ___ ___ ___ ___ ___

3 READ WORDS 5 MIN.

- Word Book page _____
- Word Cards _____

4 SPELL WORDS 7 MIN.

1. _____ _____ _____ _____ _____
2. _____ _____ _____ _____ _____
3. _____ _____ _____ _____ _____
4. _____ _____ _____ _____ _____
5. _____ _____ _____ _____ _____

- Dictate phrases or sentences

1. _____
2. _____

- Learner reads words and sentences just written.

5 READ ALOUD 10 MIN.

Book to read

Reading Strip

Board Game

Reading Level 7

MATERIALS NEEDED

- Watch Instructional Video • Sound Cards 1–23 • Sand Tray • Paper and pencil • Nerf Ball • Word Cards (pink, blue, green)
- Sight Word Cards (red) 1–5 • Word Book • Reading Marker • Reading Window and Strips 4–7 • Board Game • Book to read

1 READ SOUNDS

- Review Sound Cards **1–22**
- Learner reads sound of each card aloud.
- Go through the cards rapidly. The goal is to have automatic responses.

® Do this at the beginning of every Session.

REMINDER   Ask for clean, clipped consonant sounds. Watch Video or Audio Pronunciation CD for correct modeling of sounds.

2 SPELL SOUNDS

- Dictate the following sounds, one at a time. Dictate short vowel sounds.

    i   b   o   x   r   m   a   g

- Learner repeats the sound.
- Learner writes the letter on paper or in the sand tray.

QUESTIONS TO ASK THE LEARNER	How do you write long /a/ at the end of a word? (Answer: ay) What are two ways to write /k/? (Answer: c, k)

REMINDER   Give the sound when a slash appears on both sides of a letter. Example: /k/

BALL TOSS GAME	• Say a word while you toss or roll a Nerf Ball to the Learner.
	   Learner returns it while repeating just the middle or vowel sound of the word.
	       Example: Throw the ball and say "big"
	       Learner returns it and says, "/i/"
	 • For a list of words, see Word Book, page 9.

SONDAY SYSTEM 1 LEARNING PLAN

Reading Level 7

3 READ WORDS

5 MIN.

Learner reads aloud from the following sources. Material is provided for several Sessions.

1. Word Cards, short a, i and o (pink, blue and green, mixed).
2. Word Book, page 10, ay.
3. Word Book, page 9, Review a, i, o, x.
4. Sight Word Cards 1–5.
5. Word Book, review any previous pages.

REMINDER | If the Learner does not readily recognize a word, have the Learner trace the letters on the table and say each sound aloud, then blend the sounds into the word.

4 SPELL WORDS

7 MIN.

• Dictate the following words to the Learner.
• Learner repeats each word, <u>Touch Spells</u> each word and says each sound out loud while writing the word on paper.
• Dictate each word aloud, reading down the columns.
® Column at the far left below indicates which sound is being practiced in each row of words.
® Dictate words for seven minutes, correcting errors when they occur. Material is provided for additional Sessions.

<u>ay</u>	day	may	say	pay
<u>i</u>	six	him	pin	rip
<u>u</u>		___	___	___
<u>a</u>	lap	bag	mad	zap
<u>ay</u>	bay	lay	ray	hay
<u>o</u>	lot	top	rot	on
<u>sight</u>	the	to	is	do
<u>u</u>		___	___	___

• Learner reads the list of words just written.

• At each Session, dictate two of the following sentences.
• Learner repeats the sentence and writes it on paper.

Pat can dig a pit.   Rob can fix the box.
Tap the box top.   Dan can tag him.
Pay the cab man.   Lay it on the top.

• Check for capitalization and punctuation.

• Learner reads aloud the sentences just written.

Reading Level 7

5 INTRODUCE NEW MATERIAL 5 MIN.

1. Introduce New Sound
- Show the Card and say the sound.
- Learner repeats the sound and traces it in the sand tray.

Card: **Sound Card 23** | u | /u/ as in up

Rule: Short <u>u</u> is found at the beginning or middle of a word.

- Learner reads words from the Word Book, page 12.
- Dictate the following words.
- Learner repeats each word, <u>Touch Spells</u> each word and says each sound out loud while writing the word on paper.

> run   cup   fun   mug   bug   mud

- Learner reads the list of words just written.

® After teaching the sound, enter some of the words above in the blank spaces of ④ **SPELL WORDS.**

CORRECTING SPELLING ERRORS

- Use questions to help Learner self correct when spelling errors are made.
  When <u>cup</u> is spelled as <u>cop</u>, say,
    "<u>Touch Spell</u> that word." Wiggle the vowel finger.
    "What is the sound on this finger? How do you write it?"
- Learner rewrites the misspelled word so it is correctly spelled twice.

Reading Level 7

READ ALOUD

10 MIN.

• Choose one of the following activities at each Session.

a) Reading Strip 7.

b) Sentences, Word Book, page 13.

c) Read a book.
   - Sonday Readers, 7a, 7b, 7c. Reread 6a, 6b, 6c.
   - See page 128 of the Word Book for a list of beginning reading books.

d) Reread Reading Strips 4–6.

e) Board Game. Word Cards (pink, blue and green mixed).

HELPER'S NOTE

Good work! The key to building any skill is practice! Continue to read, write, and play games to build fluency.

Reading Level 8

MATERIALS NEEDED

- Watch Instructional Video • Sound Cards 1–24 • Sand Tray • Paper and pencil • Nerf Ball • Word Cards (pink, blue, green, yellow)
- Sight Word Cards (red) 1–8 • Word Book • Reading Marker • Reading Window and Strips 5–8 • Board Game • Book to read

---

1 READ SOUNDS

- Review Sound Cards **1–23**
- Learner reads sound of each card aloud.
- Go through the cards rapidly. The goal is to have automatic responses.

® Do this at the beginning of every Session. Reading individual letters quickly makes reading words easier.

REMINDER	Ask for two sounds of <u>a</u>, <u>i</u>, <u>o</u> and <u>u</u>, short and long. The long sound is the same as the name of the letter.

---

2 SPELL SOUNDS

- Dictate the following sounds, one at a time. Dictate short vowel sounds.

    i   d   u   r   o   p   a   x

- Learner repeats the sound.
- Learner writes the letter on paper or in the sand tray.

QUESTIONS TO ASK THE LEARNER	How do you write long /a/ at the end of a word? (Answer: ay) What are two ways to write /k/? (Answer: c, k)
BALL TOSS GAME	• Say a word while you toss or roll a Nerf Ball to the Learner. Learner returns it while repeating just the middle or vowel sound of the word. Example: Throw the ball and say "hat" Learner returns it and says, "/a/" • For a list of words, see Word Book, page 14.

SONDAY SYSTEM 1 LEARNING PLAN

Reading Level 8

3 READ WORDS

 5 MIN.

Learner reads aloud from the following sources. Material is provided for several Sessions.

1. Word Cards, short u (yellow).
2. Word Book, page 10, ay.
3. Word Cards, short a, i, o
   (pink, blue and green, mixed).
4. Word Book, page 12, Short u.
5. Word Book, page 14, Review a, i, o, u.
6. Sight Word Cards 1–5.
7. Word Book, review any previous pages.

REMINDER | Practicing words over and over builds fluency.

4 SPELL WORDS

 7 MIN.

- Dictate the following words to the Learner.
- Learner repeats each word, <u>Touch Spells</u> each word and says each sound out loud while writing the word on paper.
- Dictate each word aloud, reading down the columns.
- ® Column at the far left below indicates which sound is being practiced in each row of words.
- ® Dictate words for seven minutes, correcting errors when they occur. Material is provided for additional Sessions.

<u>u</u>	cup	mud	fun	rug
<u>ay</u>	bay	hay	lay	day
<u>o</u>	mop	dot	jog	rot
<u>ee</u>		___	___	___
<u>i</u>	hit	fin	rim	tip
<u>a</u>	sad	rag	van	am
<u>ee</u>		___	___	___
<u>sight</u>		___	___	___

- Learner reads the list of words just written.

- At each Session, dictate two of the following sentences.
- Learner repeats the sentence and writes it on paper.

Sam can run to the bay.	The pup is in the box.
Do not hit the cat.	Pat can hug the pup.
Fix the rug.	It is hot in the sun.

- Check for capitalization and punctuation.
- Learner reads aloud the sentences just written.

Reading Level 8

5 INTRODUCE NEW MATERIAL 5 MIN.

1. Introduce New Sight Words
- Teach the following Sight Words, one in each Session.
- These words cannot be sounded out and need to be memorized.

Card: **Sight Word Cards 6-8** | I | of | and |

- Show the Learner one Sight Word Card, say it aloud and ask the Learner to repeat it.
- Learner traces the letters on the table while saying the letter names.
- Learner repeats the word before and after tracing.
- Learner writes new Sight Word on paper.

® After teaching, enter these words in the blank spaces of ④ **SPELL WORDS,** to dictate during the next Session.

2. Introduce New Sound
- Show the Card and say the sound.
- Learner repeats the sound and traces it in the sand tray.

Card: **Sound Card 24** | ee | /ee/ as in deep

Rule: ee is the first choice for the long sound of e in the middle of a word.

- Learner reads words from the Word Book, page 15.

- Dictate the following words.
- Learner repeats each word, Touch Spells each word and says each sound out loud while writing the word on paper.

meet   feed   see   feet   seem   deep

- Learner reads the list of words just written.

® After teaching the sound, enter some of the words above in the blank spaces of ④ **SPELL WORDS.**

CORRECTING SPELLING ERRORS
- Use questions to help Learner self correct when spelling errors are made.
  When feed is spelled as fed, ask,
    "What is the vowel sound?"
    "How do you spell that sound in the middle of a word?"
- Learner rewrites the misspelled word so it is correctly spelled twice.

SONDAY SYSTEM 1 LEARNING PLAN

Reading Level 8

READ ALOUD

10 MIN.

- Choose one of the following activities at each Session.

a) Reading Strip 8.

b) Sentences, Word Book, page 16.

c) Read a book.
   - Sonday Readers, 8a, 8b, 8c. Reread 7a, 7b, 7c.
   - See page 128 of the Word Book for a list of beginning reading books.

d) Reread Reading Strips 5-7.

e) Board Game. Word Cards (pink, blue, green and yellow mixed).

HELPER'S NOTE	Seeing, hearing and feeling letter shapes and sounds will weld them into memory.

Reading Level 9

MATERIALS NEEDED

- Watch Instructional Video • Sound Cards 1–25 • Sand Tray • Paper and pencil • Nerf Ball • Word Cards (pink, blue, green, yellow, orange)
- Sight Word Cards (red) 1–8 • Word Book • Reading Marker • Reading Window and Strips 6–9 • Board Game • Book to read

---

1 READ SOUNDS 2 MIN.

- Review Sound Cards **1–24**
- Learner reads sound of each card aloud.
- Go through the cards rapidly. The goal is to have automatic responses.

® Do this at the beginning of every Session.

REMINDER	Mix the Sound Cards.

---

2 SPELL SOUNDS 2 MIN.

- Dictate the following sounds, one at a time. Dictate short vowel sounds.

  o   b   a   i   g   m   u   f

- Learner repeats the sound.
- Learner writes the letter on paper or in the sand tray.

QUESTIONS TO ASK THE LEARNER	How do you write long /e/ in the middle of a word? (Answer: ee) How do you spell long /a/ at the end of a word? (Answer: ay)

BALL TOSS GAME	• Say a word while you toss or roll a Nerf Ball to the Learner.
	   Learner returns it while repeating just the middle sound or vowel of the word.
	      Example: Throw the ball and say "mop"
	      Learner returns it and says, "/o/"
	• For a list of words, see Word Book, page 17.

SONDAY SYSTEM 1 LEARNING PLAN
Reading Level 9

3 READ WORDS

 5 MIN.

Learner reads aloud from the following sources. Material is provided for several Sessions.

1. Word Book, page 15, ee.
2. Word Book, page 17, Review a, i, o, u, ee, ay.
3. Word Cards, short a, i, o and u
   (pink, blue, green and yellow, mixed).
4. Word Book, page 14, Review a, i, o, u.
5. Sight Word Cards 1–8.
6. Word Cards, ay, ee (orange).
7. Word Book, page 131, Fluency practice, Level 9.

REMINDER	Reinforcement through practice builds fluency.

4 SPELL WORDS

7 MIN.

- Dictate the following words to the Learner.
- Learner repeats each word, <u>Touch Spells</u> each word and says each sound out loud while writing the word on paper.
- Dictate each word aloud, reading down the columns.
- ® Column at the far left below indicates which sound is being practiced in each row of words.
- ® Dictate words for seven minutes, correcting errors when they occur. Material is provided for additional Sessions.

<u>e</u>	___	___	___	___
<u>ee</u>	deep	seed	meet	seem
<u>i</u>	pit	sip	sit	dim
<u>ay</u>	say	ray	may	pay
<u>a</u>	fat	map	hat	rap
<u>u</u>	run	cut	bug	rub
<u>e</u>	___	___	___	___
<u>o</u>	hop	lot	cob	not
<u>sight</u>	I	of	to	

- Learner reads the list of words just written.

- At each Session, dictate two of the following sentences.
- Learner repeats the sentence and writes it on paper.

> ° I need to feed the dog.   I got a big hug.
> The seed is in the pot.   ° Jan can hop and run.
> Dan had a cup.   Don cut his lip.

- Check for capitalization and punctuation.
- Learner reads aloud the sentences just written.

Reading Level 9

INTRODUCE NEW MATERIAL   5 MIN.

5

1. Introduce New Sound
- Show the Card and say the sound.
- Learner repeats the sound and traces it in the sand tray.

Card: **Sound Card 25** | e | /e/ as in edge

Rule: Short <u>e</u> is found in the beginning or middle of a word.

- Learner reads words from the Word Book, page 18.

- Dictate the following words.
- Learner repeats each word, <u>Touch Spells</u> each word and says each sound out loud while writing the word on paper.

pet   ten   red   men   fed   set

- Learner reads the list of words just written.
- Ⓡ After teaching the sound, enter some of the words above in the blank spaces of ④ **SPELL WORDS.**

CORRECTING SPELLING ERRORS

- Use questions to help Learner self correct when spelling errors are made.
  If <u>ten</u> is spelled <u>tin</u>, ask,
      "What is the vowel sound?"
      "How do you spell that sound in the middle of a word?"
- Learner rewrites the misspelled word so it is correctly spelled twice.

Note: Be sure the Learner is pronouncing the short <u>e</u> correctly. See video demonstration.

SONDAY SYSTEM 1 LEARNING PLAN

Reading Level 9

READ ALOUD

- Choose one of the following activities at each Session.

a) Reading Strip 9.

b) Sentences, Word Book, page 19.

c) Read a book.
   - Sonday Readers, 9a, 9b, 9c. **Reread** 8a, 8b, 8c.
   - See page 128 of the Word Book for a list of beginning reading books.

d) Repeated Reading.
   From a book have the Learner read a text selection three times. Time each reading for one minute. With each repetition, the reader will read a few more words. Success and improvement are readily apparent. Rereading builds fluency.

e) Board Game. Word Cards (orange).

f) Reread Reading Strips 6–8.

HELPER'S NOTE	Point out the obvious. What seems obvious to you may not be obvious to the Learner. With everything that is taught, encourage the Learner to explain the rule, reason, or structure.
CHECK FOR MASTERY	Use Mastery Check 9, on the following page, to check progress.

Mastery Check for Reading
Use after Level 9

Using the Sonday System 1 Learning Plan format, incorporate Mastery Check for Reading in the 3. Read Words section. Have the Learner read the words aloud. Time limit is 30 seconds. If fewer than 90% of the words are read accurately, teach two more sessions and give Form B during the 3. Read Words section of the third session. Alternate Forms A and B at every third session until the Learner reaches 90%.

HELPER'S NOTE	Both Form A and B contain the same words but in a different order to avoid memorization of the sequence and require the Learner to read each word.

Have the student read the test from the Word Book, p. 140.

Reading Level 9 – Form A

met	need	tell	beef
ray	get	pay	den
dog	do	rob	of
bed	seed	jet	feet
bun	beg	bus	net

Reading Level 9 – Form B

bed	net	bus	seed
beef	tell	bun	beg
den	pay	need	met
of	rob	get	ray
feet	dog	do	jet

Count the number of words correctly read and multiply by 5 to obtain the percentage correct or use the Conversion Chart below.

CONVERSION CHART

# Correct	%	# Correct	%	# Correct	%
1	5%	8	40%	15	75%
2	10%	9	45%	16	80%
3	15%	10	50%	17	85%
4	20%	11	55%	18	90%
5	25%	12	60%	19	95%
6	30%	13	65%	20	100%
7	35%	14	70%		

The Learner should have 90% accuracy on the this test and 85% accuracy on the Spelling Mastery Check before moving to the next level.

Mastery Check for Spelling
Use after Level 9

Dictate the following words, reading down the columns. Repeat the words if necessary, but don't help the Learner make corrections. The goal is to determine what has been learned and how well the Learner can spell independently.

seem	lay	need	fed
get	zip	vet	jug
do	of	lab	feet
rob	hut	and	hop
ten	bet	sub	rib

If 17 of the 20 words have been correctly spelled proceed to the next Level.

If four or more words are misspelled categorize the errors in the columns below by marking the letter or letters which represent the correct spelling. For example:

If	seem	is spelled as	sem	mark ee
If	rob	is spelled as	rub	mark o
If	bet	is spelled as	bit	mark e
If	of	is spelled as	uv	circle of

Errors	Word Book page	Errors	Word Book page	Errors	Word Book page
b ☐	124	m ☐	125	a ☐	2,3
c ☐	124	n ☐	125	e ☐	18
d ☐	124	p ☐	125	i ☐	4
f ☐	124	r ☐	125	o ☐	5
g ☐	124	s ☐	125	u ☐	12
h ☐	124	t ☐	125	ay ☐	10
j ☐	124	v ☐	125	ee ☐	15
l ☐	124	x ☐	7		
and, of, do ☐	Sight Word	z ☐	125		

When you have identified the letters/sounds that need more practice, you may reuse Levels 7-9 or you may create Personalized Learning Plans following the instructions on the next two pages. The Word Book pages listed above will provide lists of words to use in creating learning plans. After at least four practice Sessions give this test again before moving to Level 10.

Using the form on the following page, construct a Personal Learning Plan to practice words and sounds that were missed in the Mastery Check along with words that have been mastered.

READ SOUNDS

- Use Sound Cards.
- Review all sounds that have been taught. Do this at every Session.

SPELL SOUNDS

- Use known sounds. Include those missed in the Mastery Check.
- Dictate 10 review sounds in 2 minutes or less at every Session.

READ WORDS

- Use Word Cards or Word Book lists that have been introduced.
- Read review words for 5 minutes at every Session.

SPELL WORDS

- Use words from the Word Cards or the Word Book that have been practiced. Include words that reinforce the sounds spelled incorrectly on the Mastery Check.
- Use sentences from the Word Book or create your own using words and sounds that have been taught.

READ ALOUD

- Use a Book to read, Reading Strips, or Board Game.

Learning Plan

1 READ SOUNDS 2 MIN.

- Review Sound Cards _____

2 SPELL SOUNDS 2 MIN.

_____

3 READ WORDS 5 MIN.

- Word Book page _____
- Word Cards _____

4 SPELL WORDS 7 MIN.

1. _____ _____ _____ _____ _____
2. _____ _____ _____ _____ _____
3. _____ _____ _____ _____ _____
4. _____ _____ _____ _____ _____
5. _____ _____ _____ _____ _____

- Dictate phrases or sentences

1. _____
2. _____

- Learner reads words and sentences just written.

5 READ ALOUD 10 MIN.

Book to read

Reading Strip

Board Game

Reading Level 10

MATERIALS NEEDED

- Watch Instructional Video • Sound Cards 1–27 • Sand Tray • Paper and pencil • Nerf Ball • Word Cards (pink, blue, green, yellow, purple, orange)
- Sight Word Cards (red) 1–8 • Word Book • Reading Marker • Reading Window and Strips 7–10 • Board Game • Book to read

1 READ SOUNDS

- Review Sound Cards **1–25**
- Learner reads sound of each card aloud.
- Go through the cards rapidly. The goal is to have automatic responses.

® Do this at the beginning of every Session. Reading letters quickly leads to word recognition.

REMINDER | Ask for two sounds of <u>a</u>, <u>i</u>, <u>o</u>, <u>u</u> and <u>e</u> short and long. The long sound is the same as the name of the letter.

2 SPELL SOUNDS

- Dictate the following sounds, one at a time. Dictate short vowel sounds.

  a e u d i z o

- Learner repeats the sound.
- Learner writes the letter on paper or in the sand tray.

QUESTIONS TO ASK THE LEARNER
How many ways can you spell /k/? (Answer: c, k)
How do you write long /a/ at the end of a word? (Answer: ay)
How do you spell long /e/ in the middle of a word? (Answer: ee)

BALL TOSS GAME
- Say a word while you toss or roll a Nerf Ball to the Learner.
  Learner returns it while repeating just the middle or vowel sound of the word.
      Example: Throw the ball and say "meet"
      Learner returns it and says, "/ee/"
- For a list of words, see Word Book, page 17. Use all short vowels and <u>ee</u>.

SONDAY SYSTEM 1 LEARNING PLAN

Reading Level 10

---

3 READ WORDS   5 MIN.

Learner reads aloud from the following sources. Material is provided for several Sessions.

1. Word Cards, short e (purple).
2. Word Book, page 20, Review Short Vowels.
3. Word Book, page 15, ee.
4. Word Cards, short a, i, o, u.
   (pink, blue, green, yellow).

5. Word Book, page 18, Short e.
6. Sight Word Cards 1–8.
7. Word Book, review any previous pages.

REMINDER	Practicing words over and over builds fluency.

---

4 SPELL WORDS   7 MIN.

- Dictate the following words to the Learner.
- Learner repeats each word, <u>Touch Spells</u> each word and says each sound out loud while writing the word on paper.
- Dictate each word aloud, reading down the columns.
- ® Column at the far left below indicates which sound is being practiced in each row of words.
- ® Dictate words for seven minutes, correcting errors when they occur. Material is provided for additional Sessions.

<u>e</u>	met	bet	fed	red
<u>ay</u>	day	pay	may	hay
<u>ee</u>	seed	feet	need	feel
<u>sight</u>	of	the	is	to
<u>w</u>		___	___	___
<u>a/i</u>	nap	him	tag	rip
<u>e</u>	ten	pen	let	get
<u>o/u</u>	mop	dug	log	cub
<u>y</u>		___	___	___

- Learner reads the list of words just written.

- At each Session, dictate two of the following sentences.
- Learner repeats the sentence and writes it on paper.

I can feed the red hen.	See the bug on the log.
Fix the rug.	Can I feed the pup?
I had a can of mud.	Let him run.

- Check for capitalization and punctuation.
- Learner reads aloud the sentences just written.

Reading Level 10

INTRODUCE NEW MATERIAL

1. Introduce New Sound
• Show the Card and say the sound.
• Learner repeats the sound and traces it in the sand tray.

Card: **Sound Card 26** /w/ as in wagon

• Learner reads words from the **Word Book**, page 21, column 1.

• Dictate the following words.
• Learner repeats each word, <u>Touch Spells</u> each word and says each sound out loud while writing the word on paper.

win   wax   wet   weep   wig   way

• Learner reads the list of words just written.
® After teaching the sound, enter some of the words above in the blank spaces of ④ **SPELL WORDS.**

2. Introduce New Sound
• Show the Card and say the sound.
• Learner repeats the sound and traces it in the sand tray.

Card: **Sound Card 27** /y/ as in yolk

• Learner reads words from the **Word Book**, page 21, column 2.

• Dictate the following words.
• Learner repeats each word, <u>Touch Spells</u> each word and says each sound out loud while writing the word on paper.

yes   yet   yam   yip   yap

• Learner reads the list of words just written.
® After teaching the sound, enter some of the words above in the blank spaces of ④ **SPELL WORDS.**

SONDAY SYSTEM 1 LEARNING PLAN

Reading Level 10

6 READ ALOUD

10 MIN.

• Choose one of the following activities at each Session.

a) Reading Strip 10.

b) Sentences, Word Book, page 22.

c) Read a book.
   - Sonday Readers, 10a, 10b, 10c. Reread 9a, 9b, 9c.
   - See page 128 of the Word Book for a list of beginning reading books.

d) Repeated Reading.
   From a book have the Learner read a text selection three times. Time each reading for one minute. With each repetition, the reader will read a few more words. Success and improvement are readily apparent. Rereading builds fluency.

e) Board Game. Word Cards (pink, blue, green, yellow, purple and orange, mixed).

f) Reread Reading Strips 7–9.

HELPER'S NOTE	If the sound of a letter cannot be recalled, ask the Learner to trace the letter on the table or in the sand tray. If the sound has been taught by touch, it can be recalled by touch or tracing.

Reading Level 11

MATERIALS NEEDED

- Watch Instructional Video • Sound Cards 1–28 • Sand Tray • Paper and pencil • Nerf Ball
- Word Cards (pink, blue, green, yellow, purple, orange) • Sight Word Cards (red) 1–8 • Word Book • Reading Marker
- Reading Window and Strips 8–11 • Board Game • Book to read

---

1 READ SOUNDS 2 MIN.

- Review Sound Cards **1–27**
- Learner reads sound of each card aloud.
- Go through the cards rapidly. The goal is to have automatic responses.

® Do this at the beginning of every Session.

REMINDER	Ask for two sounds of <u>a</u>, <u>i</u>, <u>o</u>, <u>u</u> and <u>e</u>, short and long.

---

2 SPELL SOUNDS 2 MIN.

- Dictate the following sounds, one at a time. Dictate short vowel sounds.

  x   a   y   e   w   o   i   u

- Learner repeats the sound.
- Learner writes the letter on paper or in the sand tray.

QUESTIONS TO ASK THE LEARNER	How do you write long /a/ at the end of a word? (Answer: ay) How do you spell long /e/ in the middle of a word? (Answer: ee)

BALL TOSS GAME	• Say a word while you toss or roll a Nerf Ball to the Learner.
	    Learner returns it while repeating just the ending sound of the word.
	       Example: Throw the ball and say "sat"
	       Learner returns it and says, "/t/"
	 • For a list of words, see Word Book, page 14.

SONDAY SYSTEM 1 LEARNING PLAN
Reading Level 11

3 READ WORDS

Learner reads aloud from the following sources. Material is provided for several Sessions.

1. Word Cards, short a, i, o, u, e
   (pink, blue, green, yellow and purple, mixed).
2. Word Book, page 23, Review Short Vowels, ee, ay.
3. Word Cards, short e (purple)
4. Word Book, page 20, Review Short Vowels.
5. Sight Word Cards 1–8.
6. Word Cards, ay, ee (orange).
7. Word Book, review any previous pages.

REMINDER	Continuous review leads to automatic responses.

4 SPELL WORDS

- Dictate the following words to the Learner.
- Learner repeats each word, <u>Touch Spells</u> each word and says each sound out loud while writing the word on paper.
- Dictate each word aloud, reading down the columns.
- ® Column at the far left below indicates which sound is being practiced in each row of words.
- ® Dictate words for seven minutes, correcting errors when they occur. Material is provided for additional Sessions.

<u>sh</u>	____	____	____	____
<u>y</u>	yes	yet	yam	yip
<u>ee</u>	beet	feed	deep	seem
<u>w</u>	win	weep	wet	wag
<u>e</u>	met	fed	set	ten
<u>sh</u>	____	____	____	____
<u>ay</u>	way	bay	lay	say
o/u	top	hut	rod	mud
a/i	lap	lip	sad	lid

- Learner reads the list of words just written.

- At each Session, dictate two of the following sentences.
- Learner repeats the sentence and writes it on paper.

May I feed the red hen?	The red wig is wet.	Did Pat get wet feet?
Mix mud in the pot.	I can feel a bug.	Did you win a cup?
I can not see Dan yet.	I can see the men.	

- Check for capitalization and punctuation.
- Learner reads aloud the sentences just written.

INTRODUCE NEW MATERIAL

5 MIN.

1. Introduce New Sound
- Show the Card and say the sound.
- Learner repeats the sound and traces it in the sand tray.

Card: **Sound Card 28** | sh | /sh/ as in ship

- Learner reads words from the Word Book, page 24.

- Dictate the following words.
- Learner repeats each word, <u>Touch Spells</u> each word and says each sound out loud while writing the word on paper.

     ship   sheep   cash   wish   shut   shed

- Learner reads the list of words just written.
- ® After teaching the sound, enter some of the words above in the blank spaces of ④ **SPELL WORDS**.

CORRECTING SPELLING ERRORS

- Use questions to help Learner self correct when spelling errors are made.
  When <u>ship</u> is spelled as <u>sip</u>, ask,
     "What is the first sound in that word?"
     "How do you spell that sound?"
- Learner rewrites the misspelled word so it is correctly spelled twice.

SONDAY SYSTEM 1 LEARNING PLAN
Reading Level 11

READ ALOUD

10 MIN.

• Choose one of the following activities at each Session.

a) Reading Strip 11.

b) Sentences, Word Book, page 25.

c) Read a book.
   - Sonday Readers. Reread 10a, 10b, 10c.
   - See page 128 of the Word Book for a list of beginning reading books.

d) Repeated Reading.
   From a book have the Learner read a text selection three times. Time each reading for one minute. With each repetition, the reader will read a few more words. Success and improvement are readily apparent. Rereading builds fluency.

e) Board Game. Word Cards (pink, blue, green, yellow, purple and orange, mixed).

f) Reread Reading Strips 8–10.

HELPER'S NOTE	Learner should say the sound aloud while writing the letter or letters. Seeing, saying-hearing, and feeling combine to cement learning.

Reading Level 12

MATERIALS NEEDED

- Watch Instructional Video • Sound Cards 1–28 • Sand Tray • Paper and pencil • Nerf Ball
- Word Cards (pink, blue, green, yellow, purple, orange) • Sight Word Cards (red) 1–8 • Word Book • Reading Marker
- Reading Window and Strips 9–12 • Board Game • Book to read

1 READ SOUNDS

- Review Sound Cards **1–28**
- Learner reads sound of each card aloud.
- Go through the cards rapidly. The goal is to have automatic responses.

® Do this at the beginning of every Session.

REMINDER	Ask for two sounds of all vowels, short and long.

2 SPELL SOUNDS

- Dictate the following sounds, one at a time. Dictate short vowel sounds.

  e   y   sh   i   a   w   o   u

- Learner repeats the sound.
- Learner writes the sound on paper or in the sand tray.

QUESTIONS TO ASK THE LEARNER	How do you write long /a/ at the end of a word? (Answer: ay)
	How do you spell long /e/ in the middle of a word? (Answer: ee)

	REMINDER	Give the sound when a slash appears on both sides of a letter. Example: /a/

BALL TOSS GAME	• Say a word while you toss or roll a Nerf Ball to the Learner.
	Learner returns it while repeating just the middle or vowel sound of the word.
	Example: Throw the ball and say "bug"
	Learner returns it and says, "/u/"
	• For a list of words, see Word Book, page 26.

SONDAY SYSTEM 1 LEARNING PLAN

Reading Level 12

3 READ WORDS

5 MIN.

Learner reads aloud from the following sources. Material is provided for several Sessions.

1. Word Cards, short e (purple).
2. Word Book, page 26, Review with sh.
3. Word Book, page 18, Short e.
4. Sight Word Cards 1-8.
5. Word Book, page 131, Fluency practice, Level 12.
6. Word Cards, short a, i, o, u, e
   (pink, blue, green, yellow and purple).
7. Word Cards, ay, ee (orange).

REMINDER | Practicing words over and over builds fluency.

4 SPELL WORDS

7 MIN.

- Dictate the following words to the Learner.
- Learner repeats each word, <u>Touch Spells</u> each word and says each sound out loud while writing the word on paper.
- Dictate each word aloud, reading down the columns.
® Column at the far left below indicates which sound is being practiced in each row of words.
® Dictate words for seven minutes, correcting errors when they occur. Material is provided for additional Sessions.

<u>sh</u>	ship	sheet	shut	shed
<u>w/y</u>	way	win	yet	yam
<u>ss</u>		___	___	___
<u>ee/ay</u>	sheep	may	weep	ray
<u>a/i</u>	bag	hid	rag	sip
<u>ll</u>				
<u>sh</u>	fish	cash	wish	dash
<u>o/u</u>	cut	mop	gum	lot
<u>ff/zz</u>		___	___	___
<u>e</u>	jet	fed	get	net

- Learner reads the list of words just written.

- At each Session, dictate two of the following sentences.
- Learner repeats the sentence and writes it on paper.

Set the dish on the top.	Dash to the top.	I wish I had the cash.
I can see ten sheep.	The red sheet is wet.	Hush up the pup.
The fish is in the dish.	May has the pot and the lid.	

- Check for capitalization and punctuation.
- Learner reads aloud the sentences just written.

5 INTRODUCE NEW MATERIAL 5 min.

1. Introduce New Sound

- Show one Card each Session and say the sound.
- Learner repeats the sound and traces it in the sand tray.

Card: **Sound Card 1** [s]   **Sound Card 5** [l]

Rule: The letters f, s, z, and l are doubled at the end of a word after a single vowel. Usually that vowel is short. This is called the 'fizzle' rule.

- Learner reads words from the Word Book, page 27.

- Dictate the following words.
- Learner repeats each word, <u>Touch Spells</u> each word and says each sound out loud while writing the word on paper.

> pass   fuss   miss   mess   boss • hill   bell   dull   well   sill

- Learner reads the list of words just written.
- ® After teaching the sound, enter some of the words above in the blank spaces of ④ **SPELL WORDS.**

CORRECTING SPELLING ERRORS

- Use questions to help Learner self correct when spelling errors are made.
  When <u>pass</u> is spelled as <u>pas</u> or <u>well</u> is spelled as <u>wel</u>, ask,
  - "What is the last sound in the word?"
  - "How do you spell that after a short vowel?"
- Learner rewrites the misspelled word so it is correctly spelled twice.

---

2. Introduce New Sound

- Show one Card each Session and say the sound.
- Learner repeats the sound and traces it in the sand tray.

Card: **Sound Card 13** [f]   **Sound Card 12** [z]

Rule: The letters f, s, z, and l are doubled at the end of a word after a single vowel. Usually that vowel is short. This is called the 'fizzle' rule.

- Learner reads words from the Word Book, page 27.

- Dictate the following words.
- Learner repeats each word, <u>Touch Spells</u> each word and says each sound out loud while writing the word on paper.

> puff   huff   doff   cuff • buzz   jazz   fuzz   fizz

- Learner reads the list of words just written.
- ® After teaching the sound, enter some of the words above in the blank spaces of ④ **SPELL WORDS.**

CORRECTING SPELLING ERRORS

- Use questions to help Learner self correct when spelling errors are made.
  When <u>puff</u> is spelled as <u>puf</u> or when <u>buzz</u> is spelled as <u>buz</u> ask,
  - "What is the last sound in that word?"
  - "How do you spell that after a short vowel?"
- Learner rewrites the misspelled word so it is correctly spelled twice.

SONDAY SYSTEM 1 LEARNING PLAN

Reading Level 12

READ ALOUD

 10 MIN.

- Choose one of the following activities at each Session.

a) Reading Strip 12.

b) Sentences, Word Book, page 28.

c) Read a Book.
   - See page 128 of the Word Book for a list of beginning reading books.

d) Repeated Reading.
   From a book have the Learner read a text selection three times. Time each reading for one minute. With each repetition, the reader will read a few more words. Success and improvement are readily apparent. Rereading builds fluency.

e) Reread Reading Strips 9–11.

f) Board Game. Word Cards (pink, blue, green, yellow, purple, and orange mixed).

HELPER'S NOTE	Reinforce relentlessly! It takes many repetitions that combine seeing, hearing, and feeling to bring the Learner to the level of automatic response.
CHECK FOR MASTERY	Use Mastery Check 12, on the following page, to check progress.

Mastery Check for Reading
Use after Level 12

Using the Sonday System 1 Learning Plan format, incorporate Mastery Check for Reading in the 3. Read Words section. Have the Learner read the words aloud. Time limit is 30 seconds. If fewer than 90% of the words are read accurately, teach two more sessions and give Form B during the 3. Read Words section of the third session. Alternate Forms A and B at every third session until the Learner reaches 90%.

HELPER'S NOTE — Both Form A and B contain the same words but in a different order to avoid memorization of the sequence and require the Learner to read each word.

Have the student read the test from the Word Book, p. 141.

Reading Level 12 – Form A

puff	mom	cuff	rut
shall	dull	wish	fell
mess	cash	fed	rush
pass	feed	moss	sheep
will	fuzz	bass	jazz

Reading Level 12 – Form B

mess	cash	wish	fell
fed	feed	pass	rush
moss	fuzz	will	sheep
mom	puff	bass	jazz
rut	shall	dull	cuff

Count the number of words correctly read and multiply by 5 to obtain the percentage correct or use the Conversion Chart below.

CONVERSION CHART

# Correct	%	# Correct	%	# Correct	%
1	5%	8	40%	15	75%
2	10%	9	45%	16	80%
3	15%	10	50%	17	85%
4	20%	11	55%	18	90%
5	25%	12	60%	19	95%
6	30%	13	65%	20	100%
7	35%	14	70%		

The Learner should have 90% accuracy on the this test and 85% accuracy on the Spelling Mastery Check before moving to the next level.

Mastery Check for Spelling
Use after Level 12

Dictate the following words, reading down the columns. Repeat the words if necessary, but don't help the Learner make corrections. The goal is to determine what has been learned and how well the Learner can spell independently.

cab	tell	mess	fox
run	cuff	rot	shop
seed	job	fuzz	deep
wet	seem	less	hush
ship	pay	wish	yet

If 17 of the 20 words have been correctly spelled proceed to the next Level.

If four or more words are misspelled categorize the errors in the columns below by marking the letter or letters which represent the correct spelling. For example:

If	ship	is spelled as	sip	mark sh
If	tell	is spelled as	tel	mark –ll
If	fox	is spelled as	foks	mark x
If	deep	is spelled as	dep	mark ee

Errors	Word Book page	Errors	Word Book page	Errors	Word Book page
b ☐	124	p ☐	125	a ☐	2, 3
c ☐	124	r ☐	125	e ☐	18
d ☐	124	s ☐	125	i ☐	4
f ☐	124	t ☐	125	o ☐	5
g ☐	124	v ☐	125	u ☐	12
h ☐	124	w ☐	21	ay ☐	10
j ☐	124	x ☐	7	ee ☐	15
l ☐	124	y ☐	21	–ff ☐	27
m ☐	125	z ☐	125	–ll ☐	27
n ☐	125	sh ☐	24	–ss ☐	27
				–zz ☐	27

When you have identified the letters/sounds that need more practice, you may reuse Levels 10–12 or you may create Personalized Learning Plans following the instructions on the next two pages. The Word Book pages listed above will provide lists of words to use in creating learning plans. After at least four practice Sessions give this test again before moving to Level 13.

Using the form on the following page, construct a Personal Learning Plan to practice words and sounds that were missed in the Mastery Check along with words that have been mastered.

READ SOUNDS

- Use Sound Cards.
- Review all sounds that have been taught. Do this at every Session.

SPELL SOUNDS

- Use known sounds. Include those missed in the Mastery Check.
- Dictate 10 review sounds in 2 minutes or less at every Session.

READ WORDS

- Use Word Cards or Word Book lists that have been introduced.
- Read review words for 5 minutes at every Session.

SPELL WORDS

- Use words from the Word Cards or the Word Book that have been practiced. Include words that reinforce the sounds spelled incorrectly on the Mastery Check.
- Use sentences from the Word Book or create your own using words and sounds that have been taught.

READ ALOUD

- Use a Book to read, Reading Strips, or Board Game.

Learning Plan

1 READ SOUNDS 2 MIN.

- Review Sound Cards _____

2 SPELL SOUNDS 2 MIN.

___ ___ ___ ___ ___ ___ ___ ___ ___ ___ ___ ___ ___ ___

3 READ WORDS 5 MIN.

- Word Book page _____
- Word Cards _____

4 SPELL WORDS 7 MIN.

1. _____ _____ _____ _____ _____
2. _____ _____ _____ _____ _____
3. _____ _____ _____ _____ _____
4. _____ _____ _____ _____ _____
5. _____ _____ _____ _____ _____

- Dictate phrases or sentences
  1. _____
  2. _____

- Learner reads words and sentences just written.

5 READ ALOUD 10 MIN.

Book to read

Reading Strip

Board Game

Reading Level 13

MATERIALS NEEDED

- Watch Instructional Video • Sound Cards 1-29 • Sand Tray • Paper and pencil • Nerf Ball
- Word Cards (pink, blue, green, yellow, purple, orange) • Sight Word Cards (red) 1-8 • Word Book • Reading Marker
- Reading Window and Strips 10-13 • Board Game • Book to read

---

1 READ SOUNDS

- Review Sound Cards **1-28**
- Learner reads sound of each card aloud.
- Go through the cards rapidly. The goal is to have automatic responses.

® Do this at the beginning of every Session.

REMINDER | Remember to shuffle Sound Cards.

---

2 SPELL SOUNDS

- Dictate the following sounds, one at a time. Dictate short vowel sounds.

  d   sh   u   o   w   i   b

- Learner repeats the sound.
- Learner writes the sound on paper or in the sand tray.

QUESTIONS TO ASK THE LEARNER	How do you spell /f/ at the end of a word after a short vowel? (Answer: ff)
	How do you spell /s/ at the end of a word after a short vowel? (Answer: ss)
	How do you write long /a/ at the end of a word? (Answer: ay)

BALL TOSS GAME	• Say a word while you toss or roll a Nerf Ball to the Learner.
	Learner returns it while repeating just the final consonant sound of the word.
	Example: Throw the ball and say "had"
	Learner returns it and says, "/d/"
	• For a list of words, see Word Book, page 26.

SONDAY SYSTEM 1 LEARNING PLAN

Reading Level 13

3 READ WORDS
5 MIN.

Learner reads aloud from the following sources. Material is provided for several Sessions.

1. Word Cards, short a, i, o, u, e
   (pink, blue, green, yellow and purple).
2. Word Book, page 30, Review with fszl.
3. Word Book, page 29, Doubling ff, ss, ll, zz.

4. Sight Word Cards 1–8.
5. Word Cards, ay, ee (orange).
6. Word Book, review any previous pages.

REMINDER | Reading words becomes easier with drill and practice.

4 SPELL WORDS
7 MIN.

- Dictate the following words to the Learner.
- Learner repeats each word, <u>Touch Spells</u> each word and says each sound out loud while writing the word on paper.
- Dictate each word aloud, reading down the columns.
- ® Column at the far left below indicates which sound is being practiced in each row of words.
- ® Dictate words for seven minutes, correcting errors when they occur. Material is provided for additional Sessions.

<u>w/y</u>	win	yes	will	yell
<u>ss</u>	miss	pass	mess	toss
<u>ee</u>	weep	sheet	meet	seed
<u>ll</u>	hill	well	sell	dull
<u>-ck</u>	___	___	___	___
<u>sh</u>	dash	hush	shed	shot
<u>ff/zz</u>	puff	jazz	huff	buzz
<u>ay</u>	pay	way	say	lay
<u>-ck</u>	___	___	___	___

- Learner reads the list of words just written.

- At each Session, dictate two of the following sentences.
- Learner repeats the sentence and writes it on paper.

Nan can not tell Bob.

I wish I had a big shell.

I need a can of gas in the jet.

Can I see the fish?

I may miss the pass.

I need to feed the sheep.

I am the boss.

Did I win the cash?

- Check for capitalization and punctuation.
- Learner reads aloud the sentences just written.

INTRODUCE NEW MATERIAL   5 MIN.

1. Introduce New Sound

- Show the Card and say the sound.
- Learner repeats the sound and traces it in the sand tray.

Card: **Sound Card 29** | -ck | /k/ as in pack

Rule: Use –ck to write the /k/ sound at the end of a word after a short vowel.

- Learner reads words from the Word Book, page 31.

- Dictate the following words.
- Learner repeats each word, <u>Touch Spells</u> each word and says each sound out loud while writing the word on paper.

   pack   deck   back   pick   duck   lick

- Learner reads the list of words just written.
- ® After teaching the sound, enter some of the words above in the blank spaces of ④ **SPELL WORDS.**

CORRECTING SPELLING ERRORS

- Use questions to help Learner self correct when spelling errors are made.
   When <u>sick</u> is spelled <u>sik</u> or <u>pack</u> is spelled as <u>pac</u>, ask,
      "What is the last sound in that word?"
      "How do you spell that after a short vowel?"
- Learner rewrites the misspelled word so it is correctly spelled twice.

SONDAY SYSTEM 1 LEARNING PLAN

Reading Level 13

READ ALOUD

 10 MIN.

• Choose one of the following activities at each Session.

a) Reading Strip 13.

b) Sentences, Word Book, page 32.

c) Reread Reading Strips 10–12.

d) Read a Book.
   – See page 128 of the Word Book for a list of beginning reading books.

e) Board Game. Word Cards (pink, blue, green, yellow, purple, and orange mixed).

HELPER'S NOTE

Praise correct answers often. Say, "Good job!", "That's right!", "Okay!", "Nice work!"

Reading Level 14

MATERIALS NEEDED

- Watch Instructional Video • Sound Cards 1–30 • Sand Tray • Paper and pencil • Nerf Ball
- Word Cards (pink, blue, green, yellow, purple, orange) • Sight Word Cards (red) 1–10 • Word Book • Reading Marker
- Reading Window and Strips 11–14 • Board Game • Book to read

---

① READ SOUNDS

- Review Sound Cards **1–29**
- Learner reads sound of each card aloud.
- Go through the cards rapidly. The goal is to have automatic responses.

® Do this at the beginning of every Session. Quick sounding and blending makes reading easier.

REMINDER	Ask for two sounds of all vowels, short and long.

---

② SPELL SOUNDS

- Dictate the following sounds, one at a time. Dictate short vowel sounds.

y   sh   a   g   i   b

- Learner repeats the sound.
- Learner writes the sound on paper or in the sand tray.

QUESTIONS TO ASK THE LEARNER	How do you spell long /e/ in the middle of a word? (Answer: ee) How do you spell /k/ after a short vowel? (Answer: -ck) How else can you spell /k/? (Answer: c and k) How do you spell /l/ after a short vowel? (Answer: ll)

BALL TOSS GAME	• Say a word while you toss or roll a Nerf Ball to the Learner.
	    Learner returns it while repeating the vowel sound of the word.
	        Example: Throw the ball and say "tap"
	        Learner returns it and says, "/a/"
	• For a list of words, see Word Book, page 24.

SONDAY SYSTEM 1 LEARNING PLAN
Reading Level 14

3 READ WORDS

5 MIN.

Learner reads aloud from the following sources. Material is provided for several Sessions.

1. Word Cards, short a, i, o, u, e
   (pink, blue, green, yellow and purple).
2. Word Book, page 30, Review with fszl.
3. Word Book, page 31, –ck.
4. Sight Word Cards 1–8.
5. Word Book, review any previous pages.

REMINDER | Practicing words over and over builds fluency.

4 SPELL WORDS

7 MIN.

- Dictate the following words to the Learner.
- Learner repeats each word, <u>Touch Spells</u> each word and says each sound out loud while writing the word on paper.
- Dictate each word aloud, reading down the columns.
- ® Column at the far left below indicates which sound is being practiced in each row of words.
- ® Dictate words for seven minutes, correcting errors when they occur. Material is provided for additional Sessions.

<u>-ck</u>	sick	back	lock	duck
<u>fszl</u>	less	puff	buzz	tell
<u>sh/ay</u>	ship	may	dish	day
<u>ee</u>	seep	sheep	need	feet
<u>fszl</u>	fuzz	toss	mill	mess
<u>-ck</u>	pack	pick	deck	shack
<u>e</u>	get	men	hen	fed
<u>qu</u>			____	____
<u>sight</u>	of	I	____	____

- Learner reads the list of words just written.

- At each Session, dictate two of the following sentences.
- Learner repeats the sentence and writes it on paper.

May can pick up the duck.	His neck is tan from the sun.
Tell Jan to get the fish.	The gull can sit on the dock.
Set the rug on the deck.	Bob had bad luck at his shack.
Lock the shack.	I can see the duck.

- Check for capitalization and punctuation.
- Learner reads aloud the sentences just written.

Reading Level 14

INTRODUCE NEW MATERIAL

1. Introduce New Sight Words
• Teach the following Sight Words, one in each Session.
• These words cannot be sounded out and need to be memorized.

Card: **Sight Word Cards 9–10** | you | | from |

• Show the Learner one Sight Word Card, say it aloud and ask the Learner to repeat it.
• Learner traces the letters on the table while saying the letter names.
• Learner repeats the word before and after tracing.
• Learner writes new Sight Word on paper.

® After teaching, enter these words in the blank spaces of ④ **SPELL WORDS,** to dictate during the next Session.

2. Introduce New Sound
• Show the Card and say the sound.
• Learner repeats the sound and traces it in the sand tray.

Card: **Sound Card 30** | qu | /kw/ as in queen

Rule: q must be followed by u.

• Learner reads words from the Word Book, page 33.
• Dictate the following words.
• Learner repeats each word, <u>Touch Spells</u> each word and says each sound out loud while writing the word on paper.

| quit | quack | quick | quill | queen | quiz |

• Learner reads the list of words just written.

® After teaching the sound, enter some of the words above in the blank spaces of ④ **SPELL WORDS.**

CORRECTING SPELLING ERRORS

• Use questions to help Learner self correct when spelling errors are made.
When <u>quit</u> is spelled as <u>qit</u> or <u>cwit</u>, ask,
"What is the first sound in that word?"
"How do you spell /kw/?"
• Learner rewrites the misspelled word so it is correctly spelled twice.

SONDAY SYSTEM 1 LEARNING PLAN

Reading Level 14

READ ALOUD

10 MIN.

• Choose one of the following activities at each Session.

a) Reading Strip 14.

b) Sentences, Word Book, page 34.

c) Reread Reading Strips 11–13.

d) Read a Book.
  – See page 128 of the Word Book for a list of beginning reading books.

e) Board Game. Word Cards (pink, blue, green, yellow, purple, and orange mixed).

HELPER'S NOTE	Only material that has been mastered will remain in long term memory.

Reading Level 15

MATERIALS NEEDED

- Watch Instructional Video • Sound Cards 1–30 • Blend Cards 1–6 • Sand Tray • Paper and pencil
- Word Cards (pink, blue, green, yellow, purple) • Sight Word Cards (red) 1–10 • Word Book • Reading Marker
- Reading Window and Strips 12–15 • Board Game • Book to read

---

1 READ SOUNDS

- Review Sound Cards **1–30**

- Learner reads sound of each card aloud.
- Go through the cards rapidly. The goal is to have automatic responses.

® Do this at the beginning of every Session.

REMINDER | Drill builds fluency.

---

2 SPELL SOUNDS

- Dictate the following sounds, one at a time. Dictate short vowel sounds.

  o   x   u   sh   qu   w

- Learner repeats the sound.
- Learner writes the sound on paper or in the sand tray.

QUESTIONS TO ASK THE LEARNER

What are three ways to spell /k/ ? (Answer: c, k, -ck)
How do you spell /f/ after a short vowel? (Answer: ff)
How do you spell /s/ after a short vowel? (Answer: ss)
How do you spell long /e/ in the middle of a word? (Answer: ee)

SONDAY SYSTEM 1 LEARNING PLAN

Reading Level 15

---

③ READ WORDS

5 MIN.

Learner reads aloud from the following sources. Material is provided for several Sessions.

1. Word Cards, short a, i, o, u, e
   (pink, blue, green, yellow and purple, mixed).
2. Word Book, page 26, Review with sh.
3. Word Book, page 31, –ck.

4. Word Book, page 35, Review –ck, fszl, qu, ee, ay.
5. Sight Word Cards 1–10.
6. Word Book, page 132, Fluency practice, Level 15.
7. Word Book, review any previous pages.

---

④ SPELL WORDS

7 MIN.

- Dictate the following words to the Learner.
- Learner repeats each word, <u>Touch Spells</u> each word and says each sound out loud while writing the word on paper.
- Dictate each word aloud, reading down the columns.
- ® Column at the far left of each set below indicates which sound is being practiced in each row of words.
- ® Dictate words for seven minutes, correcting errors when they occur. Material is provided for additional Sessions.

<u>st</u>	___	___	___	
<u>-ck</u>	sack	dock	lick	buck
<u>qu</u>	quit	quill	quick	queen
<u>sw</u>	___	___	___	
<u>fszl</u>	loss	tell	jazz	huff
<u>sc</u>	___	___	___	
<u>ee</u>	beef	seen	need	seep
<u>sight</u>	a	the	to	do
<u>ay</u>	may	hay	say	pay
<u>sp</u>	___	___	___	
<u>-ck</u>	luck	pick	tack	rock
<u>sh</u>	wish	ship	fish	sheet
<u>sm</u>	___	___	___	
<u>sn</u>	___	___	___	
<u>sight</u>	from	you	I	of

- Learner reads the list of words just written.

- At each Session, dictate two of the following sentences.
- Learner repeats the sentence and writes it on paper.

The quick cat ran.

Did the duck quack?

Dan will pick the weeds.

Jeb can feed six fish.

I will run to the bell and quit.

I need to pay cash to the man.

Did you pass the quiz?

Can you run to the hill?

Dash from the hill to the shack.

Jim may quit the job.

- Check for capitalization and punctuation.
- Learner reads aloud the sentences just written.

36

Reading Level 15

5 INTRODUCE NEW MATERIAL 5 MIN.

1. Introduce New Sound

- Introduce one blend each Session. Show the Card and say the sound.
- Learner repeats the sound and traces it in the sand tray.

Card: **Blend Card 1** | st | **Blend Card 2** | sp |

- Learner reads corresponding words from the Word Book, page 36.

- Dictate the following words.
- Learner repeats each word, <u>Touch Spells</u> each word and says each sound out loud while writing the word on paper.

stuck   stiff   steel   stuff   stay   •   speed   spin   spot   speck   spell

- Learner reads the list of words just written.
- ® After teaching the blend, enter some of the words above in the blank spaces of ④ **SPELL WORDS.**

CORRECTING SPELLING ERRORS

- Use questions to help Learner self correct when spelling errors are made.
  - When <u>stiff</u> is spelled as <u>siff</u>, say,
    - "<u>Touch Spell</u> that word"
    - "Tell me the first two sounds from your fingers."
- Learner rewrites the misspelled word so it is correctly spelled twice.

---

2. Introduce New Sound

- Introduce one blend each Session. Show the Card and say the sound.
- Learner repeats the sound and traces it in the sand tray.

Card: **Blend Card 3** | sm | **Blend Card 4** | sn |

- Learner reads corresponding words from the Word Book, page 36.

- Dictate the following words.
- Learner repeats each word, <u>Touch Spells</u> each word and says each sound out loud while writing the word on paper.

smash   smell   smock   smog   •   snap   snip   snag   snack   snug

- Learner reads the list of words just written.
- ® After teaching the blend, enter some of the words above in the blank spaces of ④ **SPELL WORDS.**

CORRECTING SPELLING ERRORS

- Use questions to help Learner self correct when spelling errors are made.
  - When <u>snap</u> is spelled as <u>sap</u>, say,
    - "<u>Touch Spell</u> that word."
    - "Tell me the first two sounds from your fingers."
- Learner rewrites the misspelled word so it is correctly spelled twice.

SONDAY SYSTEM 1 LEARNING PLAN
Reading Level 15

 5 INTRODUCE NEW MATERIAL   5 MIN.

3. Introduce New Sound
• Introduce one blend each Session. Show the Card and say the sound.
• Learner repeats the sound and traces it in the sand tray.

Card: **Blend Card 5** | sc | **Blend Card 6** | sw |

• Learner reads corresponding words from the Word Book, page 36.

• Dictate the following words.
• Learner repeats each word, <u>Touch Spells</u> each word and says each sound out loud while writing the word on paper.

scan scam scat scum scab • sweet swim sway swam swish

• Learner reads the list of words just written.
® After teaching the blend, enter some of the words above in the blank spaces of ④ **SPELL WORDS.**

CORRECTING SPELLING ERRORS	• Use questions to help Learner self correct when spelling errors are made.
	 When <u>sweet</u> is spelled as <u>seet</u>, say,
	   "<u>Touch Spell</u> that word."
	   "Tell me the first two sounds from your fingers."
	• Learner rewrites the misspelled word so it is correctly spelled twice.

 6 READ ALOUD   10 MIN.

• Choose one of the following activities at each Session.

a) Reading Strip 15.

b) Sentences, Word Book, page 37.

c) Read a Book.
   – See page 128 of the Word Book for a list of beginning reading books.

d) Repeated Reading.
   From a book have the Learner read a text selection three times. Time each reading for one minute. With each repetition, the reader will read a few more words. Rereading builds fluency.

e) Board Game. Sight Word Cards (red) 1–10.

f) Reread Reading Strips 12–14.

Mastery Check for Reading
Use after Level 15

PAGE 93

Using the Sonday System 1 Learning Plan format, incorporate Mastery Check for Reading in the 3. Read Words section. Have the Learner read the words aloud. Time limit is 30 seconds. If fewer than 90% of the words are read accurately, teach two more sessions and give Form B during the 3. Read Words section of the third session. Alternate Forms A and B at every third session until the Learner reaches 90%.

HELPER'S NOTE — Both Form A and B contain the same words but in a different order to avoid memorization of the sequence and require the Learner to read each word.

Have the student read the test from the Word Book, p. 142.

Reading Level 15 – Form A

stay	stuck	steel	stick
smash	speck	smog	spell
quill	scam	quick	scum
sweet	dish	sway	swish
snip	swell	snack	stuff

Reading Level 15 – Form B

scam	smog	spell	quill
stick	smash	speck	steel
snack	stay	stuck	stuff
sway	swell	snip	swish
quick	dish	sweet	scum

Count the number of words correctly read and multiply by 5 to obtain the percentage correct or use the Conversion Chart below.

CONVERSION CHART

# Correct	%	# Correct	%	# Correct	%
1	5%	8	40%	15	75%
2	10%	9	45%	16	80%
3	15%	10	50%	17	85%
4	20%	11	55%	18	90%
5	25%	12	60%	19	95%
6	30%	13	65%	20	100%
7	35%	14	70%		

The Learner should have 90% accuracy on the this test and 85% accuracy on the Spelling Mastery Check before moving to the next level.

Mastery Check for Spelling
Use after Level 15

Dictate the following words, reading down the columns. Repeat the words if necessary, but don't help the Learner make corrections. The goal is to determine what has been learned and how well the Learner can spell independently.

stick	spell	smash	snap
quit	scab	sheep	dash
sweet	neck	stay	swell
you	toss	spot	lock
beg	stuff	quick	hum

If 17 of the 20 words have been correctly spelled proceed to the next Level.

If four or more words are misspelled categorize the errors in the columns below by marking the letter or letters which represent the correct spelling. For example:

If	stick	is spelled as	stik	mark ck
If	smash	is spelled as	sash	mark sm
If	snap	is spelled as	snep	mark a
If	sheep	is spelled as	cheep	mark sh

Errors	Word Book page	Errors	Word Book page
a ☐	2,3	qu ☐	33
e ☐	18	y ☐	21
i ☐	4	sh ☐	24
o ☐	5	-ck ☐	31
u ☐	12	st ☐	36
ay ☐	10	sp ☐	36
ee ☐	15	sm ☐	36
-ff ☐	27	sn ☐	36
-ll ☐	27	sc ☐	36
-ss ☐	27	sw ☐	36
-zz ☐	27	you ☐	Sight Word

When you have identified the letters/sounds that need more practice, you may reuse Levels 13–15 or you may create Personalized Learning Plans following the instructions on the next two pages. The Word Book pages listed above will provide lists of words to use in creating learning plans. After at least four practice Sessions give this test again before moving to Level 16.

Using the form on the following page, construct a Personal Learning Plan to practice words and sounds that were missed in the Mastery Check along with words that have been mastered.

---

1 READ SOUNDS

- Use Sound Cards.
- Review all sounds that have been taught. Do this at every Session.

---

2 SPELL SOUNDS

- Use known sounds. Include those missed in the Mastery Check.
- Dictate 10 review sounds in 2 minutes or less at every Session.

---

3 READ WORDS

- Use Word Cards or Word Book lists that have been introduced.
- Read review words for 5 minutes at every Session.

---

4 SPELL WORDS

- Use words from the Word Cards or the Word Book that have been practiced. Include words that reinforce the sounds spelled incorrectly on the Mastery Check.
- Use sentences from the Word Book or create your own using words and sounds that have been taught.

---

5 READ ALOUD

- Use a Book to read, Reading Strips, or Board Game.

Learning Plan

1 READ SOUNDS 2 MIN.

- Review Sound Cards _____

2 SPELL SOUNDS 2 MIN.

___ ___ ___ ___ ___ ___ ___ ___ ___ ___

3 READ WORDS 5 MIN.

- Word Book page _____
- Word Cards _____

4 SPELL WORDS 7 MIN.

1. _____ _____ _____ _____
2. _____ _____ _____ _____
3. _____ _____ _____ _____
4. _____ _____ _____ _____
5. _____ _____ _____ _____

- Dictate phrases or sentences

1. _____
2. _____

Learner reads words and sentences just written.

5 READ ALOUD 10 MIN.

Book to read

Reading Strip

Board Game

MATERIALS NEEDED

- Watch Instructional Video • Sound Cards 1–30 • Blend Cards 1–12 • Sand Tray • Paper and pencil
- Word Cards (pink, blue, green, yellow, purple, tan 1) • Sight Word Cards (red) 1–10 • Word Book • Reading Marker
- Reading Window and Strips 13–16 • Board Game • Book to read

① READ SOUNDS
2 MIN.

- Review Sound Cards **1–30**

- Review Blend Cards **1–6**

- Learner reads sound of each card aloud.
- Go through the cards rapidly. The goal is to have automatic responses.

® Do this at the beginning of every Session.

REMINDER   Consonant sounds should be clean and clipped.

② SPELL SOUNDS
2 MIN.

- Dictate the following sounds, one at a time. Dictate short vowel sounds.

  u   st   sw   sh   qu   sp   o   sm   e

- Learner repeats the sound.
- Learner writes the sound on paper or in the sand tray.

QUESTIONS TO ASK THE LEARNER

How do you spell /l/ after a short vowel? (Answer: ll)

® Give the sound when a slash appears on both sides of a letter. Example: /l/.

SONDAY SYSTEM 1 LEARNING PLAN
Reading Level 16

---

3 READ WORDS

5 MIN.

Learner reads aloud from the following sources. Material is provided for several Sessions.

1. Word Book, page 38, Review S blends, qu.
2. Word Book, page 35, Review -ck, fszl, qu, ee, ay.
3. Word Cards, s blends (tan 1).

4. Word Cards, short a, i, o, u, e
   (pink, blue, green, yellow and purple, mixed).
5. Sight Word Cards 1–10.
6. Word Book, review any previous pages.

4 SPELL WORDS

7 MIN.

- Dictate the following words to the Learner.
- Learner repeats each word, <u>Touch Spells</u> each word and says each sound out loud while writing the word on paper.
- Dictate each word aloud, reading down the columns.
- ® Column at the far left of each set below indicates which sound is being practiced in each row of words.
- ® Dictate words for seven minutes, correcting errors when they occur.

<u>cl</u>		___	___	___
<u>st/sw</u>	step	sweet	stuck	swim
<u>gl</u>		___	___	___
<u>qu</u>	quick	quiz	quit	queen
<u>bl</u>		___	___	___
<u>sc/sp</u>	scat	speed	scan	spell
<u>sh/-ck</u>	smash	stack	shop	speck
<u>fl</u>		___	___	___
<u>ee</u>	feet	sweep	steep	beef
<u>ay</u>	sway	bay	stay	ray
<u>pl</u>		___	___	___
<u>sm/sn</u>	smell	snap	smock	snug
<u>sl</u>		___	___	___

- Learner reads the list of words just written.

- At each Session, dictate two of the following sentences.
- Learner repeats the sentence and writes it on paper.

I see a quick red fox.

Feed the mush to the pig.

The dish is in the box.

Van will sleep well.

Swim to the step.

I can tell Rick and Jeff.

Pass the cash to him.

Tell Stan to run.

Can Nick spot the sheep?

Snap the box shut.

- Check for capitalization and punctuation.
- Learner reads aloud the sentences just written.

Reading Level 16

5 INTRODUCE NEW MATERIAL

1. Introduce New Sound

- Introduce one blend each Session. Show the Card and say the sound.
- Learner repeats the sound and traces it in the sand tray.

Card: **Blend Card 7** bl   **Blend Card 8** cl

- Learner reads corresponding words from the Word Book, page 39.

- Dictate the following words.
- Learner repeats each word, <u>Touch Spells</u> each word and says each sound out loud while writing the word on paper.

black   block   blot   bless   bleed   •   clip   clock   clam   clap   clay

- Learner reads the list of words just written.
- ® After teaching the blend, enter some of the words above in the blank spaces of ④ **SPELL WORDS.**

CORRECTING SPELLING ERRORS

- Use questions to help Learner self correct when spelling errors are made.
  When <u>black</u> is spelled as <u>back</u>, say,
  "<u>Touch Spell</u> that word."
  "Tell me the first two sounds from your fingers."
- Learner rewrites the misspelled word so it is correctly spelled twice.

---

2. Introduce New Sound

- Introduce one blend each Session. Show the Card and say the sound.
- Learner repeats the sound and traces it in the sand tray.

Card: **Blend Card 9** fl   **Blend Card 10** pl

- Learner reads corresponding words from the Word Book, page 40.

- Dictate the following words.
- Learner repeats each word, <u>Touch Spells</u> each word and says each sound out loud while writing the word on paper.

flap   flush   flock   flax   fleet   •   plan   plum   plot   plush   plug

- Learner reads the list of words just written.
- ® After teaching the blend, enter some of the words above in the blank spaces of ④ **SPELL WORDS.**

CORRECTING SPELLING ERRORS

- Use questions to help Learner self correct when spelling errors are made.
  When <u>flock</u> is spelled as <u>lock</u>, say,
  "<u>Touch Spell</u> that word."
  "Tell me the first two sounds from your fingers."
- Learner rewrites the misspelled word so it is correctly spelled twice.

SONDAY SYSTEM 1 LEARNING PLAN

Reading Level 16

5 INTRODUCE NEW MATERIAL

5 MIN.

3. Introduce New Sound

• Introduce one blend each Session. Show the Card and say the sound.

• Learner repeats the sound and traces it in the sand tray.

Card: **Blend Card 11** gl   **Blend Card 12** sl

• Learner reads corresponding words from the Word Book, page 40.

• Dictate the following words.

• Learner repeats each word, <u>Touch Spells</u> each word and says each sound out loud while writing the word on paper.

glad   glass   gloss   glib   glob • slip   slam   slash   slot   slush

• Learner reads the list of words just written.

® After teaching the blend, enter some of the words above in the blank spaces of ④ **SPELL WORDS.**

6 READ ALOUD

10 MIN.

• Choose one of the following activities at each Session.

a) Reading Strip 16.

b) Sentences, Word Book, page 41.

c) Reread Reading Strips 13–15.

d) Read a Book.
   – See page 128 of the Word Book for a list of beginning reading books.

e) Board Game. Word Cards (tan 1).

| HELPER'S NOTE | When an error is made, using positive questions instead of negative responses will encourage the Learner to keep trying and to self-correct. |

Reading Level 17

MATERIALS NEEDED

- Watch Instructional Video • Sound Cards 1–30 • Blend Cards 1–19 • Sand Tray • Paper and pencil
- Word Cards (tan 1–2) • Sight Word Cards (red) 1–10 • Word Book • Reading Marker
- Reading Window and Strips 14–17 • Board Game • Book to read

1 READ SOUNDS

2 MIN.

- Review Sound Cards **1–30**
- Review Blend Cards **1–12**

- Learner reads sound of each card aloud.
- Go through the cards rapidly. The goal is to have automatic responses.

® Do this at the beginning of every Session.

REMINDER | Ask for two sounds of all single vowels.

2 SPELL SOUNDS

2 MIN.

- Dictate the following sounds, one at a time.

fl   qu   gl   d   e   pl   sp   sl

- Learner repeats the sound.
- Learner writes the sound on paper or in the sand tray.

QUESTIONS TO ASK THE LEARNER | How many different ways can you spell /k/? (Answer: c, k, –ck)
How do you spell long /a/ at the end of a word? (Answer: ay)

SONDAY SYSTEM 1 LEARNING PLAN
Reading Level 17

---

③ READ WORDS

5 MIN.

Learner reads aloud from the following sources. Material is provided for several Sessions.

1. Word Book, page 39, bl, cl.
2. Word Book, page 36, S Blends.
3. Word Book, page 42, Review with Blends.
4. Word Book, page 40, fl, pl, gl, sl.
5. Word Cards, Beginning Blends (tan 1–2).
6. Sight Word Cards 1–10.
7. Word Book, review any previous pages.
8. Ball Toss Game, Beginning Blends, Word Book, page 38.

---

④ SPELL WORDS

7 MIN.

• Dictate the following words to the Learner.
• Learner repeats each word, <u>Touch Spells</u> each word and says each sound out loud while writing the word on paper.
• Dictate each word aloud, reading down the columns.
® Column at the far left of each set below indicates which sound is being practiced in each row of words.
® Dictate words for seven minutes, correcting errors when they occur.

<u>cr</u>	___	___	___	
<u>st/sl</u>	stiff	slot	steep	slip
<u>tr</u>	___	___	___	
<u>ee/ay</u>	speed	stay	weep	play
<u>bl/fl</u>	bluff	fleet	bleed	fluff
<u>fr</u>	___	___	___	
<u>qu/ll</u>	quack	swell	quill	still
<u>fl/gl</u>	flag	glad	flock	glass
<u>dr</u>	___	___	___	
<u>-ck</u>	stuck	slick	block	black
<u>br</u>	___	___	___	
<u>pl/cl</u>	plum	clock	plan	click
<u>pr</u>	___	___	___	
<u>sh</u>	rush	mash	shell	gash
<u>gr</u>	___	___	___	

• Learner reads the list of words just written.

• At each Session, dictate two of the following sentences.
• Learner repeats the sentence and writes it on paper.

The flock of ducks will stop at the bay.

Set the clock.

The black pig can not see you.

Stay on top of the stack.

I see clams and fish in the dish.

A speck of gum is on the box.

The van is still stuck in the mud.

Hit the deck.

Let Glen see the plan.

Dan has a stiff leg.

• Check for capitalization and punctuation.
• Learner reads aloud the sentences just written.

5 INTRODUCE NEW MATERIAL 5 MIN.

1. Introduce New Sound

- Introduce one blend each Session. Show the Card and say the sound.
- Learner repeats the sound and traces it in the sand tray.

Card: **Blend Card 13** `cr`   **Blend Card 14** `tr`

- Learner reads corresponding words from the Word Book, page 43.

- Dictate the following words.
- Learner repeats each word, <u>Touch Spells</u> each word and says each sound out loud while writing the word on paper.

crush   crib   crab   creep   crop • trap   trick   trash   tray   trim

- Learner reads the list of words just written.
- ℞ After teaching the blend, enter some of the words above in the blank spaces of ④ **SPELL WORDS.**

CORRECTING SPELLING ERRORS

- Use questions to help Learner self correct when spelling errors are made.
    If <u>crush</u> is spelled as <u>krush</u>, ask,
        "What is the first sound in this word?"
        "What is your first choice for /k/ at the beginning of a word?"
- Learner rewrites the misspelled word so it is correctly spelled twice.
- ℞ <u>K</u> is used at the beginning of a word only before <u>e</u>, <u>i</u> and <u>y</u>.

2. Introduce New Sound

- Introduce one blend each Session. Show the Card and say the sound.
- Learner repeats the sound and traces it in the sand tray.

Card: **Blend Card 15** `fr`   **Blend Card 16** `dr`

- Learner reads corresponding words from the Word Book, page 43.

- Dictate the following words.
- Learner repeats each word, <u>Touch Spells</u> each word and says each sound out loud while writing the word on paper.

frog   fresh   frill   frock   free • drop   dress   drug   drill   drip

- Learner reads the list of words just written.
- ℞ After teaching the blend, enter some of the words above in the blank spaces of ④ **SPELL WORDS.**

CORRECTING SPELLING ERRORS

- Use questions to help Learner self correct when spelling errors are made.
    If <u>fresh</u> is spelled as <u>fesh</u>, say,
        "<u>Touch Spell</u> that word."
        Wiggle the /r/ finger. "What's the sound on this finger?"
- Learner rewrites the misspelled word so it is correctly spelled twice.

SONDAY SYSTEM 1 LEARNING PLAN
Reading Level 17

INTRODUCE NEW MATERIAL
5 MIN.

3. Introduce New Sound
- Introduce one blend each Session. Show the Card and say the sound.
- Learner repeats the sound and traces it in the sand tray.

Card: **Blend Card 17** br   **Blend Card 18** pr   **Blend Card 19** gr

- Learner reads corresponding words from the Word Book, page 44.

- Dictate the following words.
- Learner repeats each word, <u>Touch Spells</u> each word and says each sound out loud while writing the word on paper.

brick bran brass brag • press prim prom prop • grab grass greet gri

- Learner reads the list of words just written.

Ⓡ After teaching the blend, enter some of the words above in the blank spaces of ④ **SPELL WORDS.**

CORRECTING SPELLING ERRORS
- Use questions to help Learner self correct when spelling errors are made.
  If <u>brick</u> is spelled as <u>drick</u>, say,
    "Hands up! What's the first sound in brick?"
    "Which hand shows that sound? Trace the <u>b</u> and say /b/. "
- Learner rewrites the misspelled word so it is correctly spelled twice.

READ ALOUD
10 MIN.

- Choose one of the following activities at each Session.

a) Reading Strip 17.

b) Sentences, Word Book, page 45.

c) Reread Reading Strips 14–16.

d) Read a Book.
  - See page 128 of the Word Book for a list of beginning reading books.

e) Board Game. Word Cards (tan 1–2).

HELPER'S NOTE
Memory is strengthened by seeing, hearing and feeling. This is called multisensory instruction and it is essential to making the Sonday System 1 work.

Reading Level 18

MATERIALS NEEDED

- Watch Instructional Video • Sound Cards 1–30 • Blend Cards 1–19 • Sand Tray • Paper and pencil
- Word Cards (tan 1–3) • Sight Word Cards (red) 1–14 • Word Book • Reading Marker
- Reading Window and Strips 15–18 • Board Game • Book to read

1 READ SOUNDS

- Review Sound Cards **1–30**
- Review Blend Cards **1–19**

- Learner reads sound of each card aloud.
- Go through the cards rapidly. The goal is to have automatic responses.

® Do this at the beginning of every Session.

REMINDER Shuffle the Sound Cards. Shuffle the Blend Cards.

2 SPELL SOUNDS

- Dictate the following sounds, one at a time.

a   fr   e   gr   i   tr   o   cr   u   pr

- Learner repeats the sound.
- Learner writes the sound on paper or in the sand tray.

SONDAY SYSTEM 1 LEARNING PLAN
Reading Level 18

3 READ WORDS

5 MIN.

Learner reads aloud from the following sources. Material is provided for several Sessions.

1. Word Book, page 46, Review sh, –ck, qu, fszl.
2. Word Book, page 43, cr, tr, fr, dr.
3. Word Book, page 47, Review with Beginning Blends.
4. Word Book, page 44, br, pr, gr.

5. Word Book, page 132, Fluency practice, Level 18.
6. Sight Word Cards 1–10.
7. Word Cards, Beginning Blends (tan 1–3).
8. Word Book, review any previous pages.

4 SPELL WORDS

7 MIN.

- Dictate the following words to the Learner.
- Learner repeats each word, <u>Touch Spells</u> each word and says each sound out loud while writing the word on paper.
- Dictate each word aloud, reading down the columns.
® Column at the far left below indicates which sound is being practiced in each row of words.
® Dictate words for seven minutes, correcting errors when they occur. Material is provide for additional Sessions.

<u>tr/gr</u>	trip	grill	trust	grim
<u>cr</u>	crash	cram	crush	creep
<u>y</u>		____	____	____
<u>ee/ay</u>	steep	clay	sheet	tray
<u>ss/ff</u>	class	cliff	cross	bluff
<u>sight</u>	you		____	____
<u>-ck</u>	pluck	click	wick	speck
<u>fr/dr</u>	fresh	drop	frog	dress
<u>long vowel</u>		____	____	____
<u>qu/sh</u>	quill	cash	quick	sheep
<u>br/pr</u>	brim	press	brat	prop
<u>long vowel</u>		____	____	____

- Learner reads the list of words just written.

- At each Session, dictate two of the following sentences.
- Learner repeats the sentence and writes it on paper.

Do not step on the track.

Play a trick on Pam.

Set a trap for the rat.

Press the dress.

Get a snack at the club.

I had a fresh plum.

Did you drop the clay?

He cut the green grass.

A frog swam in the bay.

Play the drum at the prom.

- Check for capitalization and punctuation.
- Learner reads aloud the sentences just written.

5 INTRODUCE NEW MATERIAL 5 MIN.

1. Introduce New Sight Words
• Teach the following Sight Words, one in each Session.
• These words cannot be sounded out and need to be memorized.

Card: **Sight Word Cards 11–14** | are | | was | | who | | what |

• Show the Learner one Sight Word Card, say it aloud and ask the Learner to repeat it.
• Learner traces the letters on the table while saying the letter names.
• Learner repeats the word before and after tracing.
• Learner writes new Sight Word on paper.
® After teaching, enter these words in the blank spaces of ④ **SPELL WORDS,** to dictate during the next Session.

2. Introduce New Sound
• Show the Card and say the sound.
• Learner repeats the sound and traces it in the sand tray.

Card: **Sound Card 27** | y |　long /i/ as in by

Rule: When y comes at the end of a short word, it has the sound of long /i/.

• Learner reads words from the Word Book, page 48.

• Dictate the following words.
• Learner repeats each word, <u>Touch Spells</u> each word and says each sound out loud while writing the word on paper.

by　my　shy　fly　cry　dry　fry　spy

• Learner reads the list of words just written.
® After teaching the sound, enter some of the words above in the blank spaces of ④ **SPELL WORDS.**

CORRECTING SPELLING ERRORS
• Use questions to help Learner self correct when spelling errors are made.
When <u>fly</u> is spelled as <u>fli</u>, ask,
　　"What is the last sound in that word?"
　　"How do you spell the long /i/ sound at the end of a word?"
• Learner rewrites the misspelled word so it is correctly spelled twice.

SONDAY SYSTEM 1 LEARNING PLAN
Reading Level 18

5 INTRODUCE NEW MATERIAL

3. Introduce New Sound

• Show the Card and say the sound.
• Learner repeats the sound and traces it in the sand tray.

Card: **Sound Card 25** e   **Sound Card 20** o

Rule: The <u>e</u> or <u>o</u> at the end of short words will usually be long sounds.
(Exceptions are <u>to</u> and <u>do</u> which we have had as Sight Words.)

• Learner reads words from the Word Book, page 48.

• Dictate the following words.
• Learner repeats each word, <u>Touch Spells</u> each word and says each sound out loud while writing the word on paper.

me   he   we   she   be   •   no   go   so

• Learner reads the list of words just written.
℞ After teaching the sound, enter some of the words above in the blank spaces of ④ **SPELL WORDS.**

6 READ ALOUD

• Choose one of the following activities at each Session.

a) Reading Strip 18.

b) Sentences, Word Book, page 49.

c) Read a Book.
 – See page 128 of the Word Book for a list of beginning reading books.

d) Repeated Reading.
 From a book have the Learner read a text selection three times. Time each reading for one minute. With each repetition, the reader will read a few more words. Rereading builds fluency.

e) Board Game. Sight Word Cards (tan 1–3).

f) Reread Reading Strips 15–17.

HELPER'S NOTE	When there is difficulty reading a letter or a word, have the Learner trace the letters in the word. Sounds that have been taught by tracing, can often be retrieved by tracing. When there is difficulty spelling a word, have the Learner <u>Touch Spell</u>. Sounds that have been taught separately can be identified more easily when they are separated.

Mastery Check for Reading
Use after Level 18

Using the Sonday System 1 Learning Plan format, incorporate Mastery Check for Reading in the 3. Read Words section. Have the Learner read the words aloud. Time limit is 30 seconds. If fewer than 90% of the words are read accurately, teach two more sessions and give Form B during the 3. Read Words section of the third session. Alternate Forms A and B at every third session until the Learner reaches 90%.

HELPER'S NOTE
Both Form A and B contain the same words but in a different order to avoid memorization of the sequence and require the Learner to read each word.

Have the student read the test from the Word Book, p. 143.

Reading Level 18 – Form A

my	trash	shy	brick
stem	cry	swim	dry
she	smell	we	scab
bless	crop	clash	free
go	flat	so	slam

Reading Level 18 – Form B

so	slam	she	smell
bless	shy	brick	crop
dry	swim	go	flat
trash	we	scab	my
free	stem	cry	clash

Count the number of words correctly read and multiply by 5 to obtain the percentage correct or use the Conversion Chart below.

CONVERSION CHART

# Correct	%	# Correct	%	# Correct	%
1	5%	8	40%	15	75%
2	10%	9	45%	16	80%
3	15%	10	50%	17	85%
4	20%	11	55%	18	90%
5	25%	12	60%	19	95%
6	30%	13	65%	20	100%
7	35%	14	70%		

The Learner should have 90% accuracy on the this test and 85% accuracy on the Spelling Mastery Check before moving to the next level.

Mastery Check for Spelling
Use after Level 18

Dictate the following words, reading down the columns. Repeat the words if necessary, but don't help the Learner make corrections. The goal is to determine what has been learned and how well the Learner can spell independently.

snack	quill	brass	truck
bleed	play	speck	clay
smell	fish	stuff	queen
clock	drop	from	click
gray	sheet	sweep	fly

If 17 of the 20 words have been correctly spelled proceed to the next Level.

If four or more words are misspelled categorize the errors in the columns below by marking the letter or letters which represent the correct spelling. For example:

If	brass	is spelled as	bass	mark br
If	play	is spelled as	pay	mark pl
If	smell	is spelled as	sell	mark sm
If	stuff	is spelled as	stuf	mark –ff

Errors	Word Book page	Errors	Word Book page	Errors	Word Book page
a ☐	2, 3	sh ☐	24	pl ☐	40
e ☐	18	–ck ☐	31	gl ☐	40
i ☐	4	qu ☐	33	sl ☐	40
o ☐	5	st ☐	36	cr ☐	43
u ☐	12	sp ☐	36	tr ☐	43
ay ☐	10	sm ☐	36	fr ☐	43
ee ☐	15	sn ☐	36	dr ☐	43
–ff ☐	27	sc ☐	36	br ☐	44
–ll ☐	27	sw ☐	36	pr ☐	44
–ss ☐	27	bl ☐	39	gr ☐	44
–zz ☐	27	cl ☐	39	y ☐	49
		fl ☐	40	from ☐	Sight Word

When you have identified the letters/sounds that need more practice, you may reuse Levels 16–18 or you may create Personalized Learning Plans following the instructions on the next two pages. The Word Book pages listed above will provide lists of words to use in creating learning plans. After at least four practice Sessions give this test again before moving to Level 19.

Creating A Personal Learning Plan

Using the form on the following page, construct a Personal Learning Plan to practice words and sounds that were missed in the Mastery Check along with words that have been mastered.

READ SOUNDS

- Use Sound Cards.
- Review all sounds that have been taught. Do this at every Session.

SPELL SOUNDS

- Use known sounds. Include those missed in the Mastery Check.
- Dictate 10 review sounds in 2 minutes or less at every Session.

READ WORDS

- Use Word Cards or Word Book lists that have been introduced.
- Read review words for 5 minutes at every Session.

SPELL WORDS

- Use words from the Word Cards or the Word Book that have been practiced. Include words that reinforce the sounds spelled incorrectly on the Mastery Check.
- Use sentences from the Word Book or create your own using words and sounds that have been taught.

READ ALOUD

- Use a Book to read, Reading Strips, or Board Game.

Learning Plan

1 READ SOUNDS 2 MIN.

- Review Sound Cards _____

2 SPELL SOUNDS 2 MIN.

_____

3 READ WORDS 5 MIN.

- Word Book page _____
- Word Cards _____

4 SPELL WORDS 7 MIN.

1. _____ _____ _____ _____
2. _____ _____ _____ _____
3. _____ _____ _____ _____
4. _____ _____ _____ _____
5. _____ _____ _____ _____

- Dictate phrases or sentences

1. _____
2. _____

- Learner reads words and sentences just written.

5 READ ALOUD 10 MIN.

Book to read

Reading Strip

Board Game

Reading Level 19

MATERIALS NEEDED

- Watch Instructional Video • Sound Cards 1–31 • Blend Cards 1–19 • Sand Tray • Paper and pencil
- Word Cards (tan 1–3) • Sight Word Cards (red) 1–14 • Word Book • Reading Marker
- Reading Window and Strips 16–19 • Board Game • Book to read

1 READ SOUNDS

- Review Sound Cards **1–30**
- Review Blend Cards **1–19**
- Learner reads sound of each card aloud.
- Go through the cards rapidly. The goal is to have automatic responses.

® Do this at the beginning of every Session.

REMINDER   Ask for two sounds of all vowels and y̲.

2 SPELL SOUNDS

- Dictate the following sounds, one at a time.

gl   tr   sl   u   e   br

- Learner repeats the sound.
- Learner writes the sound on paper or in the sand tray.

QUESTIONS TO ASK THE LEARNER

How do you spell long /i/ at the end of a word? (Answer: y)
How do you spell /k/ after a short vowel? (Answer: –ck)
How else can you spell /k/? (Answer: c and k)
How do you spell long /a/ at the end of a word? (Answer: ay)

SONDAY SYSTEM 1 LEARNING PLAN
Reading Level 19

3 READ WORDS

🕐 5 MIN.

Learner reads aloud from the following sources. Material is provided for several Sessions.

1. Word Cards, Beginning Blends (tan 1–3).
2. Word Book, page 50, Review with Vowel Endings.
3. Sight Word Cards 1–14.
4. Word Book, page 46, Review with sh, –ck, qu, fszl.

5. Word Book, page 152, Level 19, Nonsense Words.
6. Word Book, review any previous pages.
7. Ball Toss Game, Beginning Blends, Word Book, page 42.

---

4 SPELL WORDS

🕐 7 MIN.

- Dictate the following words to the Learner.
- Learner repeats each word, <u>Touch Spells</u> each word and says each sound out loud while writing the word on paper.
- Dictate each word aloud, reading down the columns.
- ® Column at the far left below indicates which sound is being practiced in each row of words.
- ® Dictate words for seven minutes, correcting errors when they occur.

long vowel	go	no	so	we
cr/tr	crop	trap	crash	trim
y	my	shy	fly	spy
ch		___	___	___
long vowel	me	be	he	she
ee/ay	bleed	way	sweet	gray
fr/dr	frock	drip	free	drill
st/sl	stem	sleep	step	slush
ch		___	___	___
sh/-ck	shush	track	clash	truck
y	by	dry	cry	fry
sight	are	was	who	what

- Learner reads the list of words just written.

- At each Session, dictate two of the following sentences.
- Learner repeats the sentence and writes it on paper.

We can go to class.

Can you meet us at the track?

Did you set my clock?

We will run to the cliff.

Tell me if she will fly on the trip.

She had a red dress.

I will fry the fish.

No way!

Fran is a pro.

- Check for capitalization and punctuation.
- Learner reads aloud the sentences just written.

INTRODUCE NEW MATERIAL

5

1. Introduce New Sound

• Show the Card and say the sound.

• Learner repeats the sound and traces it in the sand tray.

Card: **Sound Card 31** | ch | /ch/ as in chip

• Learner reads words from the Word Book, page 51.

• Dictate the following words.

• Learner repeats each word, <u>Touch Spells</u> each word and says each sound out loud while writing the word on paper.

chip   chin   chill   chop   chick   chap   check

• Learner reads the list of words just written.

® After teaching the sound, enter some of the words above in the blank spaces of ④ **SPELL WORDS.**

CORRECTING SPELLING ERRORS

• Use questions to help Learner self correct when spelling errors are made.

When <u>chip</u> is spelled as <u>ship</u>, ask,

    "What is the first sound in that word?"

    "How do you spell /ch/?"

• Learner rewrites the misspelled word so it is correctly spelled twice.

SONDAY SYSTEM 1 LEARNING PLAN

Reading Level 19

READ ALOUD

10 MIN.

- Choose one of the following activities at each Session.

a) Reading Strip 19.

b) Sentences, Word Book, page 52.

c) Reread Reading Strips 16–18.

d) Read a Book.
  – See page 128 of the Word Book for a list of beginning reading books.

e) Board Game. Word Cards (tan 1–3).

HELPER'S NOTE	Allow the Learner 'think time' before writing a sound or a word. Sometimes silent rehearsal comes before a response.

MATERIALS NEEDED

- Watch Instructional Video • Sound Cards 1-33 • Blend Cards 1-19 • Sand Tray • Paper and pencil
- Word Cards (tan 1-3) • Sight Word Cards (red) 1-14 • Word Book • Reading Marker
- Reading Window and Strips 17-20 • Board Game • Book to read

---

1 READ SOUNDS

2 MIN.

- Review Sound Cards **1-31**

- Review Blend Cards **1-19**

- Learner reads sound of each card aloud.
- Go through the cards rapidly. The goal is to have automatic responses.

® Do this at the beginning of every Session.

REMINDER | Mix the Blend Cards.

---

2 SPELL SOUNDS

2 MIN.

- Dictate the following sounds, one at a time.

  u   ch   i   pl   e   y   sp   tr

- Learner repeats the sound.
- Learner writes the sound on paper or in the sand tray.

QUESTIONS TO ASK THE LEARNER

How do you spell long /i/ at the end of a word? (Answer: y)
How do you spell long /e/ in the middle of a word? (Answer: ee)

SONDAY SYSTEM 1 LEARNING PLAN
Reading Level 20

3 READ WORDS

5 MIN.

Learner reads aloud from the following sources. Material is provided for several Sessions.

1. Word Book, page 47, Review with Beginning Blends.
2. Word Cards, Beginning Blends (tan 1-3).
3. Word Book, page 51, ch.
4. Word Book, page 50, Review with Vowel Endings.

5. Sight Word Cards 1-14.
6. Word Book, page 152, Level 20, Nonsense Words.
7. Word Book, review any previous pages.

4 SPELL WORDS

7 MIN.

- Dictate the following words to the Learner.
- Learner repeats each word, <u>Touch Spells</u> each word and says each sound out loud while writing the word on paper.
- Dictate each word aloud, reading down the columns.
® Column at the far left below indicates which sound is being practiced in each row of words.
® Dictate words for seven minutes, correcting errors when they occur.

<u>ch</u>	chip	chill	chop	chick
<u>long vowel</u>	go	we	so	he
<u>sight</u>	are	was	who	what
<u>dr/tr/cr/fr</u>	drop	tree	crick	free
<u>or</u>		___	___	___
<u>ay/ee</u>	clay	speed	way	creep
<u>ch</u>	chin	much	rich	such
<u>all</u>		___	___	___
<u>or</u>		___	___	___
<u>sh/-ck</u>	mesh	trick	shell	shock
<u>y</u>	cry	dry	fly	shy
<u>all</u>		___	___	___

- Learner reads the list of words just written.

- At each Session, dictate two of the following sentences.
- Learner repeats the sentence and writes it on paper.

Who was in the class?

Are you in the truck?

He was at the crash.

Who has a green dress?

Jan will chat with me.

The chick can not fly yet.

My speech is by the bench.

Dad can chop the tree.

Did you check on the class?

Can my chum play chess?

- Check for capitalization and punctuation.
- Learner reads aloud the sentences just written.

Reading Level 20

5 INTRODUCE NEW MATERIAL 5 MIN.

1. Introduce New Sound

- Show the Card and say the sound.
- Learner repeats the sound and traces it in the sand tray.

Card: **Sound Card 32** | or | /or/ as in corn

- Learner reads words from the Word Book, page 53.

- Dictate the following words.
- Learner repeats each word, <u>Touch Spells</u> each word and says each sound out loud while writing the word on paper.

| corn | short | fort | born | sport | horn | sort |

- Learner reads the list of words just written.
- ® After teaching the sound, enter some of the words above in the blank spaces of ④ **SPELL WORDS.**

CORRECTING SPELLING ERRORS

- Use questions to help Learner self correct when spelling errors are made.
  When <u>short</u> is spelled as <u>shrot</u>, underline the <u>ro</u>. Ask,
      "What is this sound?"
      "How do you spell that sound?"
- Learner rewrites the misspelled word so it is correctly spelled twice.

---

2. Introduce New Sound

- Show the Card and say the sound.
- Learner repeats the sound and traces it in the sand tray.

Card: **Sound Card 33** | all | /all/ as in ball

- Learner reads words from the Word Book, page 53.

- Dictate the following words.
- Learner repeats each word, <u>Touch Spells</u> each word and says each sound out loud while writing the word on paper.

| ball | tall | wall | fall | call | hall | small |

- Learner reads the list of words just written.
- ® After teaching the sound, enter some of the words above in the blank spaces of ④ **SPELL WORDS.**

SONDAY SYSTEM 1 LEARNING PLAN

Reading Level 20

6 READ ALOUD

10 MIN.

- Choose one of the following activities at each Session.

a) Reading Strip 20.

b) Sentences, Word Book, page 54.

c) Reread Reading Strips 17–19.

d) Read a Book.
   – See page 128 of the Word Book for a list of beginning reading books.

e) Board Game. Word Cards (tan 1–3).

| HELPER'S NOTE | Praise and encourage neat, legible handwriting. |

MATERIALS NEEDED

- Watch Instructional Video • Sound Cards 1–34 • Blend Cards 1–19 • Sand Tray • Paper and pencil • Nerf Ball
- Word Cards (tan 1–3) • Sight Word Cards (red) 1–17 • Word Book • Reading Marker
- Reading Window and Strips 18–21 • Board Game • Book to read

---

1 READ SOUNDS

- Review Sound Cards **1–33** (every Session)

- Review Blend Cards **1–19** (every 2nd Session)

- Learner reads sound of each card aloud.
- Go through the cards rapidly. The goal is to have automatic responses.

REMINDER | Practice cements learning.

---

2 SPELL SOUNDS

- Dictate the following sounds, one at a time.

  e   or   ch   cr   tr   y   all   bl

- Learner repeats the sound.
- Learner writes the sound on paper or in the sand tray.

QUESTIONS TO ASK THE LEARNER |
How do you spell long /i/ at the end of a word? (Answer: y)
How do you spell /s/ after a short vowel? (Answer: ss)

SONDAY SYSTEM 1 LEARNING PLAN
Reading Level 21

3 READ WORDS

 5 MIN.

Learner reads aloud from the following sources. Material is provided for several Sessions.

1. Word Book, page 51, ch.
2. Word Book, page 53, or, all.
3. Word Book, page 55, Review with or, all, ch.
4. Sight Word Cards 1–14.

5. Word Cards, Beginning Blends (tan 1–3).
6. Word Book, page 133, Fluency practice, Level 21.
7. Word Book, any previous pages.
8. Ball Toss Game, Beginning Blends, Word Book, page 47.

4 SPELL WORDS

 7 MIN.

- Dictate the following words to the Learner.
- Learner repeats each word, <u>Touch Spells</u> each word and says each sound out loud while writing the word on paper.
- Dictate each word aloud, reading down the columns.
- ® Column at the far left below indicates which sound is being practiced in each row of words.
- ® Dictate words for seven minutes, correcting errors when they occur.

<u>ch</u>	chat	chess	chum	check
<u>all</u>	ball	stall	small	wall
<u>long vowel</u>	no	we	she	be
<u>sight</u>	what	was	are	who
<u>th</u>		____		____
<u>dr/tr/cr/fr</u>	drill	trap	crush	frog
<u>bl/cl/fl/sl</u>	bleed	clap	flash	sleep
<u>th</u>		____	____	____
<u>sight</u>	from	____	____	____
<u>or</u>	short	form	sport	born
<u>sh/-ck</u>	dish	click	short	track
<u>or</u>	horn	sort	fort	storm

- Learner reads the list of words just written.

- At each Session, dictate two of the following sentences.
- Learner repeats the sentence and writes it on paper.

Pat is so small.

Tom is tall and I am short.

I can see the storm.

Who is the man in the hall?

Get a cord for the box.

The corn is tall.

Toss the ball at the wall.

Dad can chop the tree.

The ship is not in port.

Play the brass horn.

- Check for capitalization and punctuation.
- Learner reads aloud the sentences just written.

INTRODUCE NEW MATERIAL

1. Introduce New Sight Words
- Teach the following Sight Words, one in each Session.
- These words cannot be sounded out and need to be memorized.

Card: **Sight Word Cards 15-17** | your | | said | | were |

- Show the Learner one Sight Word Card, say it aloud and ask the Learner to repeat it.
- Learner traces the letters on the table while saying the letter names.
- Learner repeats the word before and after tracing.
- Learner writes new Sight Word on paper.

® After teaching, enter these words in the blank spaces of ④ **SPELL WORDS**, to dictate during the next Session.

2. Introduce New Sound
- Show the Card and say the sound.
- Learner repeats the sound and traces it in the sand tray.

Card: **Sound Card 34** | th | /th/ as in thumb or that

Rule: <u>th</u> has two sounds, one voiced and one unvoiced. Practice them separately only if the Learner seems confused.

- Learner reads words from the Word Book, page 56.

- Dictate the following words.
- Learner repeats each word, <u>Touch Spells</u> each word and says each sound out loud while writing the word on paper.

thin   with   that   thick   math   then   them

- Learner reads the list of words just written.

® After teaching the sound, enter some of the words above in the blank spaces of ④ **SPELL WORDS**.

SONDAY SYSTEM 1 LEARNING PLAN

Reading Level 21

6 READ ALOUD

10 MIN.

• Choose one of the following activities at each Session.

a) Reading Strip 21.

b) Sentences, Word Book, page 57.

c) Read a Book.
  – See page 128 of the Word Book for a list of beginning reading books.

d) Repeated Reading.
   From a book have the Learner read a text selection three times. Time each reading for one minute. With each repetition, the reader will read a few more words. Success and improvement are readily apparent. Rereading builds fluency.

e) Reread Reading Strips 18–20.

f) Board Game. Sight Word Cards (red) 1–17.

HELPER'S NOTE	Feel free to repeat dictated words or sentences if the Learner asks to have something repeated.
CHECK FOR MASTERY	Use Mastery Check 21, on the following page, to check progress.

Mastery Check for Reading
Use after Level 21

Using the Sonday System 1 Learning Plan format, incorporate Mastery Check for Reading in the 3. Read Words section. Have the Learner read the words aloud. Time limit is 30 seconds. If fewer than 90% of the words are read accurately, teach two more sessions and give Form B during the 3. Read Words section of the third session. Alternate Forms A and B at every third session until the Learner reaches 90%.

HELPER'S NOTE Both Form A and B contain the same words but in a different order to avoid memorization of the sequence and require the Learner to read each word.

Have the student read the test from the Word Book, p. 144.

Reading Level 21 – Form A

thick	me	cloth	no
chop	them	chess	thorn
fly	ball	fry	small
path	you	with	what
fork	stork	storm	plug

Reading Level 21 – Form B

small	fry	you	path
thorn	chess	ball	fly
no	cloth	them	chop
storm	thick	me	plug
with	stork	fork	what

Count the number of words correctly read and multiply by 5 to obtain the percentage correct or use the Conversion Chart below.

CONVERSION CHART

# Correct	%	# Correct	%	# Correct	%
1	5%	8	40%	15	75%
2	10%	9	45%	16	80%
3	15%	10	50%	17	85%
4	20%	11	55%	18	90%
5	25%	12	60%	19	95%
6	30%	13	65%	20	100%
7	35%	14	70%		

The Learner should have 90% accuracy on the this test and 85% accuracy on the Spelling Mastery Check before moving to the next level.

Mastery Check for Spelling
Use after Level 21

Dictate the following words, reading down the columns. Repeat the words if necessary, but don't help the Learner make corrections. The goal is to determine what has been learned and how well the Learner can spell independently.

sport	path	form	grim
was	small	what	shed
thin	fleet	stall	chill
green	plum	clock	track
fluff	shock	fork	bled

If 17 of the 20 words have been correctly spelled proceed to the next Level.

If four or more words are misspelled categorize the errors in the columns below by marking the letter or letters which represent the correct spelling. For example:

If	sport	is spelled as	sprot	mark or
If	thin	is spelled as	tin	mark th
If	stall	is spelled as	stal	mark –ll
If	bled	is spelled as	bleed	mark e

Errors	Word Book page	Errors	Word Book page	Errors	Word Book page
a ☐	2,3	st ☐	36	cr ☐	43
e ☐	18	sp ☐	36	tr ☐	43
i ☐	4	sm ☐	36	fr ☐	43
o ☐	5	sn ☐	36	dr ☐	43
u ☐	12	sc ☐	36	br ☐	44
ay ☐	10	sw ☐	36	pr ☐	44
ee ☐	15	bl ☐	39	gr ☐	44
–ff ☐	27	cl ☐	39	or ☐	53
–ll ☐	27	fl ☐	40	all ☐	53
sh ☐	24	pl ☐	40	th ☐	56
–ck ☐	31	gl ☐	40	was ☐	Sight Word
		sl ☐	40	what ☐	Sight Word

When you have identified the letters/sounds that need more practice, you may reuse Levels 19 – 21 or you may create Personalized Learning Plans following the instructions on the next two pages. The Word Book pages listed above will provide lists of words to use in creating learning plans. After at least four practice Sessions give this test again before moving to Level 22.

Creating A Personal Learning Plan

Using the form on the following page, construct a Personal Learning Plan to practice words and sounds that were missed in the Mastery Check along with words that have been mastered.

1 READ SOUNDS

- Use Sound Cards.
- Review all sounds that have been taught. Do this at every Session.

2 SPELL SOUNDS

- Use known sounds. Include those missed in the Mastery Check.
- Dictate 10 review sounds in 2 minutes or less at every Session.

3 READ WORDS

- Use Word Cards or Word Book lists that have been introduced.
- Read review words for 5 minutes at every Session.

4 SPELL WORDS

- Use words from the Word Cards or the Word Book that have been practiced. Include words that reinforce the sounds spelled incorrectly on the Mastery Check.
- Use sentences from the Word Book or create your own using words and sounds that have been taught.

5 READ ALOUD

- Use a Book to read, Reading Strips, or Board Game.

Learning Plan

① READ SOUNDS   2 MIN.

• Review Sound Cards _____

② SPELL SOUNDS   2 MIN.

___ ___ ___ ___ ___ ___ ___ ___ ___ ___ ___ ___ ___ ___

③ READ WORDS   5 MIN.

• Word Book page _____

• Word Cards _____

④ SPELL WORDS   7 MIN.

1. _____ _____ _____ _____
2. _____ _____ _____ _____
3. _____ _____ _____ _____
4. _____ _____ _____ _____
5. _____ _____ _____ _____

• Dictate phrases or sentences

1. _____
2. _____

• Learner reads words and sentences just written.

⑤ READ ALOUD   10 MIN.

Book to read

Reading Strip

Board Game

Reading Level 22

MATERIALS NEEDED

- Watch Instructional Video • Sound Cards 1–35 • Blend Cards 1–19 • Sand Tray • Paper and pencil
- Word Cards (tan 1–3) • Sight Word Cards (red) 1–17 • Word Book • Reading Marker
- Reading Window and Strips 19–22 • Board Game • Book to read

1 READ SOUNDS

- Review Sound Cards **1–34** (every Session)

- Review Blend Cards **1–19** (every 3rd Session)

- Learner reads sound of each card aloud.
- Go through the cards rapidly. The goal is to have automatic responses.

REMINDER   Ask for two sounds of all vowels and y.

2 SPELL SOUNDS

- Dictate the following sounds, one at a time.

sl   sp   all   fr   th   or   qu   gr   cl   e

- Learner repeats the sound.
- Learner writes the sound on paper or in the sand tray.

SONDAY SYSTEM 1 LEARNING PLAN
Reading Level 22

3 READ WORDS

5 MIN.

Learner reads aloud from the following sources. Material is provided for several Sessions.

1. Word Book, page 58, Review with th, sh, ch.
2. Word Book, page 55, Review with or, all, ch.
3. Sight Word Cards 1–17.
4. Word Book, Page 153, Level 22, Nonsense Words.
5. Word Cards, Beginning Blends (tan 1–3).
6. Word Book, review any previous pages.

4 SPELL WORDS

7 MIN.

- Dictate the following words to the Learner.
- Learner repeats each word, <u>Touch Spells</u> each word and says each sound out loud while writing the word on paper.
- Dictate each word aloud, reading down the columns.
- ® Column at the far left below indicates which sound is being practiced in each row of words.
- ® Dictate words for seven minutes, correcting errors when they occur.

<u>th</u>	thick	thin	with	path
<u>all</u>	fall	tall	mall	stall
<u>ing</u>		___	___	___
<u>sight</u>	you	were	your	said
<u>dr/tr/cr/fr</u>	drug	truck	crop	frill
<u>ang</u>		___	___	___
<u>bl/cl/fl/sl</u>	block	club	flush	slush
<u>th</u>	them	this	then	math
<u>ong</u>		___	___	___
<u>or</u>	corn	torn	form	short
<u>ch</u>	chin	porch	check	chuck
<u>ung</u>		___	___	___

- Learner reads the list of words just written.

- At each Session, dictate two of the following sentences.
- Learner repeats the sentence and writes it on paper.

What did you do?

Go to your math class.

What sport do you play?

Mom said we can stay.

Who is up in your tree?

That black pig is thin.

Pat is stuck by the wall.

Were you with them?

Dad and Mom are at the mall.

Dry the dish with a thick cloth.

- Check for capitalization and punctuation.
- Learner reads aloud the sentences just written.

Reading Level 22

⑤ INTRODUCE NEW MATERIAL　⏱ 5 MIN.

1. Introduce New Sound

- Show the Card and say the sound.
- Learner repeats the sound and traces it in the sand tray.

Card: **Sound Card 35** | `ing` | /ing/ as in sing

- Learner reads words from the Word Book, page 59.

- Dictate the following words.
- Learner repeats each word, <u>Touch Spells</u> each word and says each sound out loud while writing the word on paper.

　　　sing　　　ring　　　wing　　　bring　　　sting　　　thing

- Learner reads the list of words just written.
- ® After teaching the sound, enter some of the words above in the blank spaces of ④ **SPELL WORDS.**

CORRECTING SPELLING ERRORS

- Use questions to help Learner self correct when spelling errors are made.
  When <u>bring</u> is spelled as <u>brig</u>, say,
  　"I'll start the word and you finish it. /br/."
  　When <u>ing</u> has been taught as a unit, it should remain a unit. Don't break it apart.
- Learner rewrites the misspelled word so it is correctly spelled twice.

---

2. Introduce New Sound

- Show the Card and say the sound.
- Learner repeats the sound and traces it in the sand tray.

Card: **Sound Card 35** | `ang` | /ang/ as in sang

- Learner reads words from the Word Book, page 59.

- Dictate the following words.
- Learner repeats each word, <u>Touch Spells</u> each word and says each sound out loud while writing the word on paper.

　　　sang　　　bang　　　rang　　　hang　　　slang　　　gang

- Learner reads the list of words just written.
- ® After teaching the sound, enter some of the words above in the blank spaces of ④ **SPELL WORDS.**

SONDAY SYSTEM 1 LEARNING PLAN
Reading Level 22

 INTRODUCE NEW MATERIAL

3. Introduce New Sound
- Show the Card and say the sound.
- Learner repeats the sound and traces it in the sand tray.

Card: **Sound Card 35** | ong | **Sound Card 35** | ung |

- Learner reads words from the Word Book, page 59.

- Dictate the following words.
- Learner repeats each word, <u>Touch Spells</u> each word and says each sound out loud while writing the word on paper.

song   long   tong   gong   •   hung   sung   rung   stung   lung

- Learner reads the list of words just written.
- ® After teaching the sound, enter some of the words above in the blank spaces of ④ **SPELL WORDS.**

 READ ALOUD

- Choose one of the following activities at each Session.

a) Reading Strip 22.

b) Sentences, Word Book, page 60.

c) Read a Book.
   - See page 128 of the Word Book for a list of beginning reading books.

d) Reread Reading Strips 19–21.

e) Board Game. Word Cards (tan 1–3).

HELPER'S NOTE

<u>Touch Spelling</u> is magic! Ask the Learner to divide the word to be spelled into sounds using the fingers. Sounds that have been taught as units will be easily recognized when the word is broken into units.

Reading Level 23

MATERIALS NEEDED

- Watch Instructional Video • Sound Cards 1–35 • Blend Cards 1–19 • Sand Tray • Paper and pencil
- Word Cards (tan 1–3) • Sight Word Cards (red) 1–21 • Word Book • Reading Marker
- Reading Window and Strips 20–23 • Board Game • Book to read

1 READ SOUNDS

- Review Sound Cards **1–35** (every Session)

- Review Blend Cards **1–19** (every 3rd Session)

- Learner reads sound of each card aloud.
- Go through the cards rapidly. The goal is to have automatic responses.

REMINDER | Pronounce blends clearly.

2 SPELL SOUNDS

- Dictate the following sounds, one at a time.

      ing   all   ung   ch   th   ong   or   ang   qu   e

- Learner repeats the sound.
- Learner writes the sound on paper or in the sand tray.

SONDAY SYSTEM 1 LEARNING PLAN
Reading Level 23

---

③ READ WORDS

5 MIN.

Learner reads aloud from the following sources. Material is provided for several Sessions.

1. Word Book, page 59, –ng.
2. Word Book, page 61, Review or, all, –ng.
3. Sight Word Cards 1–17.

4. Word Book, Page 153, Level 23, Nonsense Words.
5. Word Cards, Beginning Blends (tan 1–3).
6. Word Book, review any previous pages.

---

④ SPELL WORDS

7 MIN.

- Dictate the following words to the Learner.
- Learner repeats each word, <u>Touch Spells</u> each word and says each sound out loud while writing the word on paper.
- Dictate each word aloud, reading down the columns.
- ® Column at the far left below indicates which sound is being practiced in each row of words.
- ® Dictate words for seven minutes, correcting errors when they occur.

<u>ing</u>	sing	thing	sting	bring
<u>all/or</u>	hall	fall	short	thorn
<u>wh</u>	___	___	___	___
<u>sight</u>	you	were	was	said
<u>dr/tr/cr/fr</u>	drip	tree	crash	fry
<u>oy</u>	___	___	___	___
<u>bl/cl/fl/sl</u>	black	cling	fling	sling
<u>th</u>	that	this	thick	path
<u>ar</u>	___	___	___	___
<u>ang</u>	sang	hang	bang	rang
<u>ch</u>	rich	chat	chop	chill
<u>ong/ung</u>	song	lung	long	sung
<u>sight</u>	your	___	___	___

- Learner reads the list of words just written.

- At each Session, dictate two of the following sentences.
- Learner repeats the sentence and writes it on paper.

The bee may sting you.

Nick had a long run up the path.

Do this math with your chum.

What is that red thing in the hall?

She said you were sick.

He sang a song for us.

Ring the bell for class.

The gang is at the mall.

Bring your math with you.

Hang it on the prong.

- Check for capitalization and punctuation.
- Learner reads aloud the sentences just written.

Reading Level 23

INTRODUCE NEW MATERIAL

1. Introduce New Sight Words
• Teach the following Sight Words, one in each Session.
• These words cannot be sounded out and need to be memorized.

Card: **Sight Word Cards 18–21** | one | only | once | does |

• Show the Learner one Sight Word Card, say it aloud and ask the Learner to repeat it.
• Learner traces the letters on the table while saying the letter names.
• Learner repeats the word before and after tracing.
• Learner writes new Sight Word on paper.
® After teaching, enter these words in the blank spaces of ④ **SPELL WORDS**, to dictate during the next Session.

2. Introduce New Sound
• Show the Card and say the sound.
• Learner repeats the sound and traces it in the sand tray.

Card: **Sound Card 36** | oy | /oy/ as in boy

Rule: <u>oy</u> is usually at the end of a word.

• Learner reads words from the Word Book, page 62.
• Dictate the following words.
• Learner repeats each word, <u>Touch Spells</u> each word and says each sound out loud while writing the word on paper.

> boy   toy   joy   Roy

• Learner reads the list of words just written.
® After teaching the sound, enter some of the words above in the blank spaces of ④ **SPELL WORDS**.

3. Introduce New Sound
• Show the Card and say the sound.
• Learner repeats the sound and traces it in the sand tray.

Card: **Sound Card 37** | ar | /ar/ as in car

• Learner reads words from the Word Book, page 62.

• Dictate the following words.
• Learner repeats each word, <u>Touch Spells</u> each word and says each sound out loud while writing the word on paper.

> car   dark   farm   yard   star   smart

• Learner reads the list of words just written.
® After teaching the sound, enter some of the words above in the blank spaces of ④ **SPELL WORDS**.

SONDAY SYSTEM 1 LEARNING PLAN
Reading Level 23

INTRODUCE NEW MATERIAL

5 MIN.

4. Introduce New Sound
• Show the Card and say the sound.
• Learner repeats the sound and traces it in the sand tray.

Card: **Sound Card 38** | wh | /wh/ as in wheel

Rule: <u>wh</u> comes at the beginning of the word. Often, <u>wh</u> and <u>w</u> sound the same.

• Learner reads words from the Word Book, page 63.

• Dictate the following words.
• Learner repeats each word, <u>Touch Spells</u> each word and says each sound out loud while writing the word on paper.

when   whip   wheel   why   wham   whiz

• Learner reads the list of words just written.
® After teaching the sound, enter some of the words above in the blank spaces of ④ **SPELL WORDS.**

CORRECTING SPELLING ERRORS

• Use questions to help Learner self correct when spelling errors are made.
  When <u>whip</u> is spelled as <u>wip</u>, ask,
    "What is the first sound in that word?"
    "How else can you spell that sound?"
• Learner rewrites the misspelled word so it is correctly spelled twice.

READ ALOUD

10 MIN.

• Choose one of the following activities at each Session.

a) Reading Strip 23.

b) Sentences, Word Book, page 64.

c) Read a Book.
   – Focus on comprehension by asking factual questions based on information that is clearly stated in the text.
      Examples: Where did she find the lost puppy?
                    When did the boy get to school?
                    What was the location of the factory?

d) Reread Reading Strips 20–22.

e) Board Game. Word Cards (tan 1–3).

Reading Level 24

MATERIALS NEEDED

- Watch Instructional Video • Sound Cards 1–40 • Blend Cards 1–19 • Sand Tray • Paper and pencil
- Word Cards (tan 1–3) • Sight Word Cards (red) 1–21 • Word Book • Reading Marker
- Reading Window and Strips 21–24 • Board Game • Book to read

---

1 READ SOUNDS

- Review Sound Cards **1–38** (every Session)

- Review Blend Cards **1–19** (every 3rd Session)

- Learner reads sound of each card aloud.
- Go through the cards rapidly. The goal is to have automatic responses.

REMINDER	Ask for two sounds of all vowels and y.

---

2 SPELL SOUNDS

- Dictate the following sounds, one at a time.

     ing   ar   ung   th   ong   bl   ang   oy   e

- Learner repeats the sound.
- Learner writes the sound on paper or in the sand tray.

QUESTIONS TO ASK THE LEARNER	What are two ways to spell /w/? (Answer: w, wh)

SONDAY SYSTEM 1 LEARNING PLAN
Reading Level 24

③ READ WORDS

5 MIN.

Learner reads aloud from the following sources. Material is provided for several Sessions.

1. Word Book, page 62, ar, oy.
2. Word Book, page 65, Review ar, -ng, oy.
3. Sight Word Cards 1–21.

4. Word Cards, Beginning Blends (tan 1–3).
5. Word Book, page 133, Fluency practice, Level 24.
6. Word Book, any previous pages.

④ SPELL WORDS

7 MIN.

- Dictate the following words to the Learner.
- Learner repeats each word, <u>Touch Spells</u> each word and says each sound out loud while writing the word on paper.
- Dictate each word aloud, reading down the columns.
® Column at the far left below indicates which sound is being practiced in each row of words.
® Dictate words for seven minutes, correcting errors when they occur.

<u>-ng</u>	gang	sung	fling	prong
<u>all/or</u>	stall	tall	storm	dorm
<u>ink</u>		___	___	___
<u>sight</u>	one	only	once	does
<u>wh</u>	when	whip	why	wheel
<u>ar/oy</u>	hard	boy	sharp	start
<u>ank</u>		___	___	___
<u>blends</u>	clock	blush	flush	slick
<u>th</u>	thin	them	cloth	thing
<u>onk/unk</u>		___	___	___
<u>ch</u>	chip	torch	chap	check
<u>oo</u>		___	___	___
<u>ar</u>	mark	yard	part	star

- Learner reads the list of words just written.

- At each Session, dictate two of the following sentences.
- Learner repeats the sentence and writes it on paper.

Roy is a smart boy.

Play with the ball in the yard.

What does the duck say?

That is a sharp thorn.

It is a joy to see you.

Only one dart hit the mark.

Do not fling the bat.

I can see a star.

This math is hard!

Which boy can go?

- Check for capitalization and punctuation.
- Learner reads aloud the sentences just written.

INTRODUCE NEW MATERIAL

5 MIN.

1. Introduce New Sound
- Show the Card and say the sound. Introduce only one new sound at a Session.
- Learner repeats the sound and traces it in the sand tray.

Card: **Sound Card 39** `ink`   **Sound Card 39** `ank`

Rule: -k is the first choice for /k/ at the end of a word after a consonant, a long vowel or a double vowel. (-ck comes only after a short vowel.)

- Learner reads words from the Word Book, page 66.

- Dictate the following words.
- Learner repeats each word, <u>Touch Spells</u> each word and says each sound out loud while writing the word on paper.

sink   wink   blink   rink   mink •   bank   sank   rank   thank   tank

- Learner reads the list of words just written.
- ® After teaching the sound, enter some of the words above in the blank spaces of ④ **SPELL WORDS.**

CORRECTING SPELLING ERRORS	• Use questions to help Learner self correct when spelling errors are made. When <u>sink</u> is spelled as <u>sick</u>, say, "Repeat the word. I'll start it, you finish it. /s/. "
	REMINDER | Keep the unit, /ink/, together as you have taught it.

2. Introduce New Sound
- Show the Card and say the sound. Introduce only one new sound at a Session.
- Learner repeats the sound and traces it in the sand tray.

Card: **Sound Card 39** `onk`   **Sound Card 39** `unk`

Rule: -k is the first choice for /k/ at the end of a word after a consonant, a long vowel or a double vowel. (-ck comes only after a short vowel.)

- Learner reads words from the Word Book, page 66.

- Dictate the following words.
- Learner repeats each word, <u>Touch Spells</u> each word and says each sound out loud while writing the word on paper.

honk   zonk   bonk •   junk   bunk   sunk   chunk   punk

- Learner reads the list of words just written.
- ® After teaching the sound, enter some of the words above in the blank spaces of ④ **SPELL WORDS.**

CORRECTING SPELLING ERRORS	• Use questions to help Learner self correct when spelling errors are made. If <u>punk</u> is spelled <u>punck</u>, ask, "When do you use <u>-ck</u>? How do you spell /k/ after a consonant?"
	REMINDER | -ck is used directly after a short vowel.

SONDAY SYSTEM 1 LEARNING PLAN
Reading Level 24

 INTRODUCE NEW MATERIAL 5 MIN.

3. Introduce New Sound
• Show the Card and say the sound.
• Learner repeats the sound and traces it in the sand tray.

Card: **Sound Card 40** | oo | /oo/ as in moon

Rule: <u>oo</u> usually comes in the middle of a word.

• Learner reads words from the Word Book, page 67.

• Dictate the following words.
• Learner repeats each word, <u>Touch Spells</u> each word and says each sound out loud while writing the word on paper.

soon   moon   food   spoon   boom   stool   hoop   boost

• Learner reads the list of words just written.
® After teaching the sound, enter some of the words above in the blank spaces of ④ **SPELL WORDS.**

CORRECTING SPELLING ERRORS

• Use questions to help Learner self correct when spelling errors are made.
When <u>stool</u> is spelled as <u>stol</u>, ask,
"What is the vowel sound in that word?" or "What is the middle sound in that word? <u>Touch Spell</u> that word."
Then say, "How do you spell that sound in the middle of a word?"
• Learner rewrites the misspelled word so it is correctly spelled twice.

 READ ALOUD 10 MIN.

• Choose one of the following activities at each Session.

a) Reading Strip 24.

b) Sentences, Word Book, page 68.

c) Read a Book.
   - See page 128 of the Word Book for a list of beginning reading books.

d) Repeated Reading.
   From a book have the Learner read a text selection three times. Time each reading for one minute. With each repetition, the reader will read a few more words. Success and improvement are readily apparent. Rereading builds fluency.

e) Board Game. Sight Word Cards (red) 1–21.

f) Reread Reading Strips 21–23.

HELPER'S NOTE

Repetition builds fluency. Let the Learner reread favorite books often.

Mastery Check for Reading
Use after Level 24

Using the Sonday System 1 Learning Plan format, incorporate Mastery Check for Reading in the 3. Read Words section. Have the Learner read the words aloud. Time limit is 30 seconds. If fewer than 90% of the words are read accurately, teach two more sessions and give Form B during the 3. Read Words section of the third session. Alternate Forms A and B at every third session until the Learner reaches 90%.

HELPER'S NOTE Both Form A and B contain the same words but in a different order to avoid memorization of the sequence and require the Learner to read each word.

Have the student read the test from the Word Book, p. 145.

Reading Level 24 – Form A

harm	wing	chart	clang
drink	speech	think	sixth
scoop	honk	gloom	junk
whiff	once	wham	does
blank	smooth	rank	broom

Reading Level 24 – Form B

smooth	blank	does	wham
once	whiff	junk	gloom
sixth	scoop	honk	think
clang	drink	speech	chart
wing	harm	rank	broom

Count the number of words correctly read and multiply by 5 to obtain the percentage correct or use the Conversion Chart below.

CONVERSION CHART

# Correct	%	# Correct	%	# Correct	%
1	5%	8	40%	15	75%
2	10%	9	45%	16	80%
3	15%	10	50%	17	85%
4	20%	11	55%	18	90%
5	25%	12	60%	19	95%
6	30%	13	65%	20	100%
7	35%	14	70%		

The Learner should have 90% accuracy on the this test and 85% accuracy on the Spelling Mastery Check before moving to the next level.

Mastery Check for Spelling
Use after Level 24

Dictate the following words, reading down the columns. Repeat the words if necessary, but don't help the Learner make corrections. The goal is to determine what has been learned and how well the Learner can spell independently.

small	blank	junk	tray
sport	smooth	toy	short
chart	starch	does	check
slang	stock	creep	droop
when	with	cliff	thing

If 17 of the 20 words have been correctly spelled proceed to the next Level.

If four or more words are misspelled categorize the errors in the columns below by marking the letter or letters which represent the correct spelling. For example:

If	chart	is spelled as	shart	mark ch
If	slang	is spelled as	slag	mark ang
If	when	is spelled as	wen	mark wh
If	smooth	is spelled as	smoth	mark oo

Errors	Word Book page	Errors	Word Book page	Errors	Word Book page
a ☐	2,3	s blends ☐	36	oy ☐	62
e ☐	18	l blends ☐	39,40	ar ☐	62
i ☐	4	r blends ☐	43,44	wh ☐	63
o ☐	5	ch ☐	51	ink ☐	66
u ☐	12	or ☐	53	ank ☐	66
ay ☐	10	all ☐	53	onk ☐	66
ee ☐	15	th ☐	56	unk ☐	66
sh ☐	24	ing ☐	59	oo ☐	67
-ck ☐	31	ang ☐	59	does ☐	Sight Word
-ff ☐	27	ong ☐	59		
		ung ☐	59		

When you have identified the letters/sounds that need more practice, you may reuse Levels 22 – 24 or you may create Personalized Learning Plans following the instructions on the next two pages. The Word Book pages listed above will provide lists of words to use in creating learning plans. After at least four practice Sessions give this test again before moving to Level 25.

Using the form on the following page, construct a Personal Learning Plan to practice words and sounds that were missed in the Mastery Check along with words that have been mastered.

1 READ SOUNDS

- Use Sound Cards.
- Review all sounds that have been taught. Do this at every Session.

2 SPELL SOUNDS

- Use known sounds. Include those missed in the Mastery Check.
- Dictate 10 review sounds in 2 minutes or less at every Session.

3 READ WORDS

- Use Word Cards or Word Book lists that have been introduced.
- Read review words for 5 minutes at every Session.

4 SPELL WORDS

- Use words from the Word Cards or the Word Book that have been practiced. Include words that reinforce the sounds spelled incorrectly on the Mastery Check.
- Use sentences from the Word Book or create your own using words and sounds that have been taught.

5 READ ALOUD

- Use a Book to read, Reading Strips, or Board Game.

Learning Plan

1 READ SOUNDS   2 MIN.

- Review Sound Cards _____

2 SPELL SOUNDS   2 MIN.

_____ _____ _____ _____ _____ _____ _____ _____ _____ _____ _____

3 READ WORDS   5 MIN.

- Word Book page _____
- Word Cards _____

4 SPELL WORDS   7 MIN.

1. _____ _____ _____ _____ _____
2. _____ _____ _____ _____ _____
3. _____ _____ _____ _____ _____
4. _____ _____ _____ _____ _____
5. _____ _____ _____ _____ _____

- Dictate phrases or sentences

1. _____
2. _____

- Learner reads words and sentences just written.

5 READ ALOUD 10 MIN.

Book to read

Reading Strip

Board Game

Reading Level 25

MATERIALS NEEDED

- Watch Instructional Video • Sound Cards 1–41 • Blend Cards 1–19 • Sand Tray • Paper and pencil
- Word Cards (tan 1–3) • Sight Word Cards (red) 1–25 • Word Book • Reading Marker
- Reading Window and Strips 22–25 • Board Game • Book to read

1 READ SOUNDS

- Review Sound Cards **1–40** (every Session)

- Review Blend Cards **1–19** (every 3rd Session)

- Learner reads sound of each card aloud.
- Go through the cards rapidly. The goal is to have automatic responses.

REMINDER Practice glues sounds and words into memory.

2 SPELL SOUNDS

- Dictate the following sounds, one at a time.

    ang   oo   ar   ink   th   ong   sh   ank   all

- Learner repeats the sound.
- Learner writes the sound on paper or in the sand tray.

QUESTIONS TO ASK THE LEARNER

How do you spell /k/ after a short vowel? (Answer: -ck)

SONDAY SYSTEM 1 LEARNING PLAN

Reading Level 25

③ READ WORDS

5 MIN.

Learner reads aloud from the following sources. Material is provided for several Sessions.

1. Word Book, page 67, oo.
2. Word Book, page 66, -nk.
3. Word Book, page 69, Review with oo, -nk.
4. Word Book, page 70, Review with -ng, oy, ar.

5. Sight Word Cards 1–21.
6. Word Cards, Beginning Blends (tan 1–3).
7. Word Book, review any previous pages.

④ SPELL WORDS

7 MIN.

• Dictate the following words to the Learner.
• Learner repeats each word, <u>Touch Spells</u> each word and says each sound out loud while writing the word on paper.
• Dictate each word aloud, reading down the columns.
® Column at the far left below indicates which sound is being practiced in each row of words.
® Dictate words for seven minutes, correcting errors when they occur.

<u>-ng</u>	bring	slang	stung	long
<u>all/or</u>	wall	hall	fort	cord
<u>wh</u>	wham	whiff	what	whisk
<u>VCe pairs</u>	___	___	___	
	___	___	___	
<u>sight</u>	were	only	your	does
<u>oo</u>	spoon	food	moon	booth
<u>-nk</u>	tank	link	chunk	honk
<u>ar</u>	chart	yarn	march	sharp
<u>VCe pairs</u>	___	___	___	
	___	___	___	
<u>oo</u>	boost	tooth	bloom	spool
<u>th</u>	thick	thin	bath	thing
<u>ch</u>	pooch	porch	starch	chick
<u>ar/oy</u>	bark	yard	joy	start

• At each Session, dictate two of the following sentences.
• Learner repeats the sentence and writes it on paper.

I had one pink dress.

Tell them to ring the bell.

Jack can sleep in his bunk.

Send the ball into the hoop.

Did you blink?

The food is in the spoon.

Toss me that glass bank.

My junk is in the shed.

When will he go?

He will play punk rock.

• Check for capitalization and punctuation.
• Learner reads aloud the sentences just written.

• Learner reads the list of words just written.

INTRODUCE NEW MATERIAL

1. Introduce New Sight Words
• Teach the following Sight Words, one in each Session.
• These words cannot be sounded out and need to be memorized.

Card: **Sight Word Cards 22–25** | two | four | done | goes |

• Show the Learner one Sight Word Card, say it aloud and ask the Learner to repeat it.
• Learner traces the letters on the table while saying the letter names.
• Learner repeats the word before and after tracing.
• Learner writes new Sight Word on paper.
® After teaching, enter these words in the blank spaces of ④ **SPELL WORDS,** to dictate during the next Session.

2. Introduce New Sound
• Show the Card and say the sound.
• Learner repeats the sound and traces it in the sand tray.

Card: **Sound Card 41**   Introduce VCe, the Vowel-Consonant-e pattern.

Rule: The <u>e</u> on the end of the word makes the preceding vowel long, (say its name).

• Learner reads words from the Word Book, page 71.

• Dictate the following words.
• Learner repeats each word, <u>Touch Spells</u> each word and says each sound out loud while writing the word on paper.

<u>Spell</u>	dim	hop	hat	pin	not
<u>make it</u>	dime	hope	hate	pine	note

• Learner reads the list of words just written.
® After teaching the sound, enter some of the words above in the blank spaces of ④ **SPELL WORDS.**

CORRECTING SPELLING ERRORS
• Use questions to help Learner self correct when spelling errors are made.
   When <u>mate</u> is spelled as <u>mat</u>, ask,
      "What kind of vowel do you have there? Long or short?"
      "How can you make the vowel long?"
• Learner rewrites the misspelled word so it is correctly spelled twice.

SONDAY SYSTEM 1 LEARNING PLAN

Reading Level 25

6 READ ALOUD

10 MIN.

- Choose one of the following activities at each Session.

a) Reading Strip 25.

b) Sentences, Word Book, page 72.

c) Read a Book.
   - Focus on comprehension by asking factual and predictive questions. Predictive questions encourage the reader to predict future action or events from the text.
      Examples: What do you think he saw?
                        How long will it take to build the wall?

d) Reread Reading Strips 22–24.

e) Board Game. Word Cards (tan 1–3).

HELPER'S NOTE	Look back at what you have accomplished. Congratulate yourselves!

Reading Level 26

MATERIALS NEEDED

- Watch Instructional Video • Sound Cards 1–41 • Blend Cards 1–25 • Sand Tray • Paper and pencil
- Word Cards (light blue) • Sight Word Cards (red) 1–27 • Word Book • Reading Marker
- Reading Window and Strips 23–27 • Board Game • Book to read

1 READ SOUNDS

- Review Sound Cards **1–41** (every Session)

- Review Blend Cards **1–19** (every 3rd Session)

- Learner reads sound of each card aloud.
- Go through the cards rapidly. The goal is to have automatic responses.

REMINDER   Reading letters quickly leads to reading words quickly.

2 SPELL SOUNDS

- Dictate the following sounds, one at a time.

     or   ank   ch   ong   oo   x

- Learner repeats the sound.
- Learner writes the sound on paper or in the sand tray.

QUESTIONS TO ASK THE LEARNER
Spell /w/ two ways. (Answer: w, wh)
Spell long /a/ three ways. (Answer: a, ay, a-e)
Spell long /i/ three ways. (Answer: i, y, i-e)
Spell long /o/ two ways. (Answer: o, o-e)

SONDAY SYSTEM 1 LEARNING PLAN
Reading Level 26

3 READ WORDS

5 MIN.

Learner reads aloud from the following sources. Material is provided for several Sessions.

1. Word Book, page 71, VCe.
2. Word Book, page 73, Review VCe.
3. Word Book, page 70, Review with –ng, oy, ar.
4. Word Book, Page 154, Level 26, Nonsense Words.

5. Word Cards, VCe (light blue).
6. Sight Word Cards 1–25.
7. Word Book, review any previous pages.

4 SPELL WORDS

 7 MIN.

- Dictate the following words to the Learner.
- Learner repeats each word, <u>Touch Spells</u> each word and says each sound out loud while writing the word on paper.
- Dictate each word aloud, reading down the columns.
- ® Column at the far left below indicates which sound is being practiced in each row of words.
- ® Dictate words for seven minutes, correcting errors when they occur.

<u>VCe</u>	mat	dim	bit	cut
	mate	dime	bite	cute
<u>-ng/-nk</u>	hung	blink	lung	junk
<u>-st</u>	___	___	___	___
<u>wh</u>	when	whiff	which	what
<u>oo</u>	coop	stool	broom	troop
<u>ar</u>	charm	shark	smart	hard
<u>-nt/-mp</u>	___	___	___	___
<u>sight</u>	two	four	done	goes
<u>-sk/-ft</u>	___	___	___	___
<u>VCe</u>	spin	mad	win	rat
	spine	made	wine	rate
<u>-nd</u>	___	___	___	___
<u>sight</u>	once	does	___	___

- Learner reads the list of words just written.

- At each Session, dictate two of the following sentences.
- Learner repeats the sentence and writes it on paper.

I did not get the note.

Can you tape it shut?

Jeff made a big slide.

I hope I can go with you.

The play is quite long.

Did you fall in the lake?

Beth will hide in the car.

Toss that stone in the creek.

Fill in the blank.

Sell it at your booth.

- Check for capitalization and punctuation.
- Learner reads aloud the sentences just written.

Reading Level 26

5 ## INTRODUCE NEW MATERIAL

5 MIN.

1. Introduce New Sight Words
• Teach the following Sight Words, one in each Session.
• These words cannot be sounded out and need to be memorized.

Card: Sight Word Cards 26–27 | there | | where |

• Show the Learner one Sight Word Card, say it aloud and ask the Learner to repeat it. Introduce only one new sight word at a Session.
• Learner traces the letters on the table while saying the letter names.
• Learner repeats the word before and after tracing.
• Learner writes new Sight Word on paper.
® After teaching, enter these words in the blank spaces of ④ **SPELL WORDS,** to dictate during the next Session.

2. Introduce New Sound
• Show the Card and say the sound. Introduce only one new sound at a Session.
• Learner repeats the sound and traces it in the sand tray.

Card: Blend Card 20 | -st | **Blend Card 21** | -nd |

• Learner reads corresponding words from the Word Book, page 74.

• Dictate the following words.
• Learner repeats each word, <u>Touch Spells</u> each word and says each sound out loud while writing the word on paper.

fast just must fist dust • sand send bond pond fund

• Learner reads the list of words just written.
® After teaching the sound, enter some of the words above in the blank spaces of ④ **SPELL WORDS.**

CORRECTING SPELLING ERRORS

• Use questions to help Learner self correct when spelling errors are made.
　When <u>sand</u> is spelled as <u>sad</u>, say,
　　"<u>Touch Spell</u> that word."
　　"What are the sounds on the last fingers?"
• Learner rewrites the misspelled word so it is correctly spelled twice.

---

3. Introduce New Sound
• Show the Card and say the sound. Introduce only one new sound at a Session.
• Learner repeats the sound and traces it in the sand tray.

Card: Blend Card 22 | -nt | **Blend Card 23** | -mp |

• Learner reads corresponding words from the Word Book, page 75.

• Dictate the following words.
• Learner repeats each word, <u>Touch Spells</u> each word and says each sound out loud while writing the word on paper.

rent mint hunt went tent • lamp stamp dump limp damp

• Learner reads the list of words just written.
® After teaching the sound, enter some of the words above in the blank spaces of ④ **SPELL WORDS.**

SONDAY SYSTEM 1 LEARNING PLAN
Reading Level 26

5 INTRODUCE NEW MATERIAL

4. Introduce New Sound
• Show the Card and say the sound. Introduce only one new sound at a Session.
• Learner repeats the sound and traces it in the sand tray.

Card: Blend Card 24 -sk   **Blend Card 25** -ft

• Learner reads corresponding words from the Word Book, page 76.

• Dictate the following words.
• Learner repeats each word, <u>Touch Spells</u> each word and says each sound out loud while writing the word on paper.

     ask   mask   risk   dusk   brisk •   left   raft   shift   craft   gift

• Learner reads the list of words just written.
® After teaching the sound, enter some of the words above in the blank spaces of ④ **SPELL WORDS.**

6 READ ALOUD

• Choose one of the following activities at each Session.

a) Reading Strip 26.

b) Sentences, Word Book, page 77.

c) Read a Book.
   - Sonday System® Readers, Level 26 a–c.
   - See page 128 of the Word Book for a list of beginning reading books.

d) Reread Reading Strips 23–25.

e) Board Game. Word Cards (light blue).

HELPER'S NOTE	Memory for words is established by using touch or 'feeling'. Tracing builds memory for words.

Reading Level 27

MATERIALS NEEDED

- Watch Instructional Video • Sound Cards 1–43 • Blend Cards 1–25 • Sand Tray • Paper and pencil
- Word Cards (light blue) • Sight Word Cards (red) 1–32 • Word Book • Reading Marker
- Reading Window and Strips 24–27 • Board Game • Book to read

1 READ SOUNDS

2 MIN.

- Review Sound Cards **1–41** (every Session)
- Review Blend Cards **1–25** (every 2nd Session)
- Learner reads sound of each card aloud.
- Go through the cards rapidly. The goal is to have automatic responses.

REMINDER | Praise quick responses.

2 SPELL SOUNDS

2 MIN.

- Dictate the following sounds, one at a time.

  ink   -mp   -ft   -nt   oy   oo   -nd

- Learner repeats the sound.
- Learner writes the sound on paper or in the sand tray.

QUESTIONS TO ASK THE LEARNER | Spell long /e/ two ways. (Answer: ee, e–e)
Spell long /a/ three ways. (Answer: a, ay, a–e)
How do you spell /f/ after a short vowel? (Answer: ff)

SONDAY SYSTEM 1 LEARNING PLAN
Reading Level 27

 **3** ## READ WORDS 5 MIN.

Learner reads aloud from the following sources. Material is provided for several Sessions.

1. Word Cards, VCe (light blue).
2. Word Book, page 73, Review VCe.
3. Word Book, page 78, Review wh, -st, -nd, -nt, etc.
4. Sight Word Cards 1–27.

5. Word Book, Page 154, Level 27, Nonsense Words.
6. Word Book, page 74–76, End Blends.
7. Word Book, page 134, Fluency practice, Level 27.
8. Word Book, review any previous pages.

4 ## SPELL WORDS 7 MIN.

- Dictate the following words to the Learner.
- Learner repeats each word, <u>Touch Spells</u> each word and says each sound out loud while writing the word on paper.
- Dictate each word aloud, reading down the columns.
- ® Column at the far left below indicates which sound is being practiced in each row of words.
- ® Dictate words for seven minutes, correcting errors when they occur.

<u>-ng/-nk</u>	cling	blank	bang	trunk
<u>VCe</u>	pin	hop	cut	tap
	pine	hope	cute	tape
<u>wh</u>	which	wham	whale	while
<u>ai</u>		___		___
<u>oo</u>	boost	fool	stoop	groom
<u>end blends</u>	pump	damp	mask	brisk
<u>ar/sight</u>	chart	where	yard	there
<u>ow</u>		___	___	___
<u>sight</u>	two	___	___	___
<u>end blends</u>	went	lint	sand	just
<u>ai</u>		___	___	___
<u>sh/ch</u>	shoot	chill	shell	chick
<u>end blends</u>	bend	trust	raft	left
<u>ow</u>		___	___	___
<u>VCe</u>	snake	drive	code	smile

- Learner reads the list of words just written.

- At each Session, dictate two of the following sentences.
- Learner repeats the sentence and writes it on paper.

Where is the tooth that you lost?

I hope the ride will be smooth.

The task is done.

Can Mark bake a cake?

Send a gift to Jan.

Sit in the shade and stay cool.

Take a ride on your bike.

Stamp the card and send it.

Just do it!

I must hunt for the list.

- Check for capitalization and punctuation.
- Learner reads aloud the sentences just written.

Reading Level 27

5 INTRODUCE NEW MATERIAL 5 MIN.

1. Introduce New Sight Words

• Teach the following Sight Words, one in each Session.

• These words cannot be sounded out and need to be memorized.

Card: **Sight Word Cards 28–32** | gone | | don't | | they | | some | | come |

• Show the Learner one Sight Word Card, say it aloud and ask the Learner to repeat it.

• Learner traces the letters on the table while saying the letter names.

• Learner repeats the word before and after tracing.

• Learner writes new Sight Word on paper.

® After teaching, enter these words in the blank spaces of ④ **SPELL WORDS,** to dictate during the next Session.

2. Introduce New Sound

• Show the Card and say the sound.

• Learner repeats the sound and traces it in the sand tray.

Card: **Sound Card 42** | o w | long /o/ as in blow

Rule: <u>ow</u> comes at the end of a word, or it may be followed by an <u>n</u>.

• Learner reads words from the Word Book, page 79.

• Dictate the following words.

• Learner repeats each word, <u>Touch Spells</u> each word and says each sound out loud while writing the word on paper.

show   blow   grow   low   bow   slow   flow   snow

• Learner reads the list of words just written.

® After teaching the sound, enter some of the words above in the blank spaces of ④ **SPELL WORDS.**

CORRECTING SPELLING ERRORS

• Use questions to help Learner self correct when spelling errors are made.

When <u>blow</u> is spelled as <u>blo</u> or <u>bloe</u>, ask,

"What do you hear at the end?"

"How can you spell long /o/ at the end of a word?"

• Learner rewrites the misspelled word so it is correctly spelled twice.

SONDAY SYSTEM 1 LEARNING PLAN

Reading Level 27

5 INTRODUCE NEW MATERIAL — 5 MIN.

3. Introduce New Sound

- Show the Card and say the sound.
- Learner repeats the sound and traces it in the sand tray.

Card: **Sound Card 43** | ai | long /a/ as in rain

Rule: The long sound of <u>a</u> is usually spelled <u>ai</u> before an <u>n</u> or an <u>l</u>.

- Learner reads words from the Word Book, page 80.

- Dictate the following words.
- Learner repeats each word, <u>Touch Spells</u> each word and says each sound out loud while writing the word on paper.

main   stain   sail   grain   faint   tail   brain   chain

- Learner reads the list of words just written.

CORRECTING SPELLING ERRORS

- Use questions to help Learner self correct when spelling errors are made.
  When <u>stain</u> is spelled as <u>stane</u>, ask,
    "What is the vowel sound in that word?"
    "How do we usually spell long /a/ before <u>n</u> or <u>l</u>?"
- Learner rewrites the misspelled word so it is correctly spelled twice.

6 READ ALOUD — 10 MIN.

- Choose one of the following activities at each Session.

a) Reading Strip 27.

b) Sentences, Word Book, page 81.

c) Read a Book.
   - Sonday System® Readers, Level 27 a–c.
   - See page 128 of the Word Book for a list of beginning reading books.

d) Repeated Reading.
   From a book have the Learner read a text selection three times. Time each reading for one minute. With each repetition, the reader will read a few more words. Success and improvement are readily apparent. Rereading builds fluency.

e) Board Game. Word Cards (light blue).

f) Reread Reading Strips 24–26.

HELPER'S NOTE

<u>Touch Spell</u> misspelled words or words involving a new sound or rule.
Easy words may be written without <u>Touch Spelling</u>.

Mastery Check for Reading
Use after Level 27

PAGE 157

Using the Sonday System 1 Learning Plan format, incorporate Mastery Check for Reading in the 3. Read Words section. Have the Learner read the words aloud. Time limit is 30 seconds. If fewer than 90% of the words are read accurately, teach two more sessions and give Form B during the 3. Read Words section of the third session. Alternate Forms A and B at every third session until the Learner reaches 90%.

HELPER'S NOTE Both Form A and B contain the same words but in a different order to avoid memorization of the sequence and require the Learner to read each word.

Have the student read the test from the Word Book, p. 146.

Reading Level 27 – Form A

champ	trust	left	spend
snow	grow	show	window
chain	gone	trail	they
where	chair	there	braid
gripe	stone	drive	flake

Reading Level 27 – Form B

chair	where	they	trail
window	chain	gone	show
grow	snow	spend	left
drive	flake	trust	champ
gripe	stone	there	braid

Count the number of words correctly read and multiply by 5 to obtain the percentage correct or use the Conversion Chart below.

CONVERSION CHART

# Correct	%	# Correct	%	# Correct	%
1	5%	8	40%	15	75%
2	10%	9	45%	16	80%
3	15%	10	50%	17	85%
4	20%	11	55%	18	90%
5	25%	12	60%	19	95%
6	30%	13	65%	20	100%
7	35%	14	70%		

The Learner should have 90% accuracy on the this test and 85% accuracy on the Spelling Mastery Check before moving to the next level.

Mastery Check for Spelling
Use after Level 27

Dictate the following words, reading down the columns. Repeat the words if necessary, but don't help the Learner make corrections. The goal is to determine what has been learned and how well the Learner can spell independently.

best	bend	hunt	limp
take	mile	vote	there
raft	brisk	stain	trail
grow	mail	snow	flow
stuck	tooth	block	smart

If 17 of the 20 words have been correctly spelled proceed to the next Level.

If four or more words are misspelled categorize the errors in the columns below by marking the letter or letters which represent the correct spelling. For example:

If	best	is spelled as	bet	mark –st
If	take	is spelled as	tack	mark VCe
If	stain	is spelled as	stane	mark ai
If	flow	is spelled as	flo	mark ow

Errors	Word Book page	Errors	Word Book page	Errors	Word Book page
a ☐	2,3	s blends ☐	36	oo ☐	67
e ☐	18	l blends ☐	39,40	VCe ☐	71
i ☐	4	r blends ☐	43,44	ow ☐	79
o ☐	5	ar ☐	62	ai ☐	80
u ☐	12	wh ☐	63	–st ☐	74
–ck ☐	31	–nd ☐	74		
ch ☐	51	–nt ☐	75		
or ☐	53	–mp ☐	75		
all ☐	53	–sk ☐	76		
th ☐	56	–ft ☐	76		
oy ☐	62	there ☐	Sight Word		

When you have identified the letters/sounds that need more practice, you may reuse Levels 25 – 27 or you may create Personalized Learning Plans following the instructions on the next two pages. The Word Book pages listed above will provide lists of words to use in creating learning plans. After at least four practice Sessions give this test again before moving to Level 28.

Creating A Personal Learning Plan

Using the form on the following page, construct a Personal Learning Plan to practice words and sounds that were missed in the Mastery Check along with words that have been mastered.

READ SOUNDS

- Use Sound Cards.
- Review all sounds that have been taught. Do this at every Session.

SPELL SOUNDS

- Use known sounds. Include those missed in the Mastery Check.
- Dictate 10 review sounds in 2 minutes or less at every Session.

READ WORDS

- Use Word Cards or Word Book lists that have been introduced.
- Read review words for 5 minutes at every Session.

SPELL WORDS

- Use words from the Word Cards or the Word Book that have been practiced. Include words that reinforce the sounds spelled incorrectly on the Mastery Check.
- Use sentences from the Word Book or create your own using words and sounds that have been taught.

READ ALOUD

- Use a Book to read, Reading Strips, or Board Game.

Learning Plan

1 READ SOUNDS   2 MIN.

- Review Sound Cards _____

2 SPELL SOUNDS   2 MIN.

— — — — — — — — — — — — — —

3 READ WORDS 5 MIN.

- Word Book page _____
- Word Cards _____

4 SPELL WORDS 7 MIN.

1. _____ _____ _____ _____ _____
2. _____ _____ _____ _____ _____
3. _____ _____ _____ _____ _____
4. _____ _____ _____ _____ _____
5. _____ _____ _____ _____ _____

- Dictate phrases or sentences
  1. _____
  2. _____

- Learner reads words and sentences just written.

5 READ ALOUD 10 MIN.

Book to read

Reading Strip

Board Game

Reading Level 28

MATERIALS NEEDED

- Watch Instructional Video • Sound Cards 1–43 • Blend Cards 1–29 • Sand Tray • Paper and pencil
- Word Cards (tan 1–3, light blue) • Sight Word Cards (red) 1–37 • Word Book • Reading Marker • Transparency and Washable Pen
- Reading Window and Strips 25–28 • Board Game • Book to read

---

1 ## READ SOUNDS

- Review Sound Cards **1–43** (every Session)

- Review Blend Cards **1–25** (every 3rd Session)

- Learner reads sound of each card aloud.
- Go through the cards rapidly. The goal is to have automatic responses.

REMINDER | Shuffle the Sound Cards and shuffle the Blend Cards.

---

2 ## SPELL SOUNDS

- Dictate the following sounds, one at a time.

pl   onk   ch   ing   ar   or   oo   th

- Learner repeats the sound.
- Learner writes the sound on paper or in the sand tray.

QUESTIONS TO ASK THE LEARNER | What are four ways to spell long /a/? (Answer: ay, a-e, a, ai)
What are three ways of spelling long /e/. (Answer: e, ee, e-e)
How do you write long /o/ at the end of a word? (Answer: ow)

SONDAY SYSTEM 1 LEARNING PLAN

Reading Level 28

③ READ WORDS

5 MIN.

Learner reads aloud from the following sources. Material is provided for several Sessions.

1. Word Book, page 79, ow.
2. Word Book, page 80, ai.
3. Word Book, page 82, Review ow, ai, VCe, oo, ee.
4. Word Book, page 83, Worksheet with –k, –ck.

5. Sight Word Cards (red) 1–32.
6. Word Cards, Beginning Blends (tan 1–3).
7. Word Cards, VCe (light blue).
8. Word Book, review any previous pages.

④ SPELL WORDS

7 MIN.

• Dictate the following words to the Learner.
• Learner repeats each word, <u>Touch Spells</u> each word and says each sound out loud while writing the word on paper.
• Dictate each word aloud, reading down the columns.
® Column at the far left below indicates which sound is being practiced in each row of words.
® Dictate words for seven minutes, correcting errors when they occur.

<u>-ng/-nk</u>	hang	blink	sung	spank
<u>VCe</u>	mine	dive	time	side
<u>wh</u>	which	when	whip	whiff
<u>compound</u>		____	____	____
<u>ai</u>	tail	jail	brain	grain
<u>oo</u>	roost	smooth	spool	troop
<u>end blends</u>	champ	stump	task	frisk
<u>ow/sight</u>	low	where	row	there
<u>end blends</u>	blend	tent	bond	fist
<u>compound</u>		____	____	____
<u>sight</u>	gone	were	don't	they
<u>ai</u>	rain	gain	stain	train
<u>sight</u>	some	____		____
<u>VCe</u>	make	save	late	cake
<u>ow</u>	show	grow	slow	blow
<u>VCe</u>	rope	tube	vote	rode

• Learner reads the list of words just written.

• At each Session, dictate two of the following sentences.
• Learner repeats the sentence and writes it on paper.

The small pink shell is gone.

I don't know where they went.

Show Dave the back yard.

Can you slide on that slope?

Wait for me by the snow drift.

The rain will fill the pail.

Hide the dark stain with paint.

We were gone when they came.

Paint the chair green.

Can you see the snow glow?

• Check for capitalization and punctuation.
• Learner reads aloud the sentences just written.

5 INTRODUCE NEW MATERIAL

5 MIN.

1. Introduce New Sight Words

• Teach the following Sight Words, one in each Session.

• These words cannot be sounded out and need to be memorized.

Card: **Sight Word Cards 33-37** | says | | want | | any | | been | | their |

• Show the Learner one Sight Word Card, say it aloud and ask the Learner to repeat it.

• Learner traces the letters on the table while saying the letter names.

• Learner repeats the word before and after tracing.

• Learner writes new Sight Word on paper.

Ⓡ After teaching, enter these words in the blank spaces of ④ **SPELL WORDS,** to dictate during the next Session.

2. Introduce Compound Words

Rule: Compound words consist of two small words that combine to make one word.

• Learner reads words from the Word Book, page 84.

• Dictate the following words.

• Learner repeats each word, breaks it into two words and writes it on paper.

sunshine   catfish   suntan   forget   popcorn   subway

• Learner reads the list of words just written.

Ⓡ After teaching, enter some of the words above in the blank spaces of ④ **SPELL WORDS.**

3. Introduce New Sound

• Show one Card each Session and say the sound.

• Learner repeats the sound and traces it in the sand tray.

Card: **Blend Card 26** | -lt | **Blend Card 27** | -lk |

• Learner reads corresponding words from the Word Book, page 85.

• Dictate the following words.

• Learner repeats each word, Touch Spells each word and says each sound out loud while writing the word on paper.

felt   tilt   melt   belt   •   milk   elk   silk   bulk

• Learner reads the list of words just written.

Ⓡ After teaching, enter some of the words above in the blank spaces of ④ **SPELL WORDS.**

CORRECTING SPELLING ERRORS

• Use questions to help Learner self correct when spelling errors are made.
   If felt is spelled as fet, say,
      "Touch Spell that word."
         Wiggle the l finger. "What is the sound on this finger?"
• Learner rewrites the misspelled word so it is correctly spelled twice.

SONDAY SYSTEM 1 LEARNING PLAN

Reading Level 28

INTRODUCE NEW MATERIAL

4. Introduce New Sound

- Show one Card each Session and say the sound.
- Learner repeats the sound and traces it in the sand tray.

Card: **Blend Card 28** **Blend Card 29**

- Learner reads corresponding words from the Word Book, page 85.

- Dictate the following words.
- Learner repeats each word, <u>Touch Spells</u> each word and says each sound out loud while writing the word on paper.

lisp   grasp   crisp   asp • act   fact   duct   sect

- Learner reads the list of words just written.

® After teaching the sound, enter some of the words above in the blank spaces of ④ **SPELL WORDS.**

READ ALOUD

- Choose one of the following activities at each Session.

a) Reading Strip 28.

b) Sentences, Word Book, page 86.

c) Read a Book.
  - Sonday System® Readers, Level 28 a–c.
  - Focus on comprehension by asking factual and predictive questions. Predictive questions encourage the reader to predict future action or events from the text.
    - Examples: What do you think he saw?
    -                How long will it take to build the wall?

d) Reread Reading Strips 25–27.

e) Board Game. Word Cards (light blue).

| HELPER'S NOTE | Praise effort and success often. Say, "Yes! Yes! Yes!"   "How about that!"   "Right on!"   "Nice!" |

Reading Level 29

MATERIALS NEEDED

- Watch Instructional Video • Sound Cards 1-43 • Blend Cards 1-29 • Sand Tray • Paper and pencil
- Word Cards(light blue, gold) • Sight Word Cards (red) 1-37 • Word Book • Reading Marker • Transparency and Washable Pen
- Reading Window and Strips 26-28 • Board Game • Book to read

1 READ SOUNDS

- Review Sound Cards **1-43** (every Session)

- Review Blend Cards **1-29** (every 3rd Session)

- Learner reads sound of each card aloud.
- Go through the cards rapidly. The goal is to have automatic responses.

REMINDER | Ask for two sounds of all vowels and y.

2 SPELL SOUNDS

- Dictate the following sounds, one at a time.

  -ft   ank   ch   ar   sh   oo   -ct

- Learner repeats the sound.
- Learner writes the sound on paper or in the sand tray.

QUESTIONS TO ASK THE LEARNER | What are three ways of spelling long /e/. (Answer: ee, e-e, e)
How do you write long /o/ at the end of a word? (Answer: ow)
How do you write long /a/ before n or l? (Answer: ai)

SONDAY SYSTEM 1 LEARNING PLAN
Reading Level 29

 **3** ## READ WORDS

 5 MIN.

Learner reads aloud from the following sources. Material is provided for several Sessions.

1. Word Book, page 87, Review ai, ow, VCe, Compounds, End Blends.
2. Word Book, page 84, Compound Words 1.
3. Word Book, page 88, Review -k, -ck, -ke.
4. Word Book, page 89, Worksheet with -k, -ck, -ke.

5. Sight Word Cards (red) 1–37.
6. Word Cards, VCe (light blue).
7. Word Cards, End Blends (gold).
8. Word Book, review any previous pages.

4 ## SPELL WORDS

 7 MIN.

- Dictate the following words to the Learner.
- Learner repeats each word, <u>Touch Spells</u> each word and says each sound out loud while writing the word on paper.
- Dictate each word aloud, reading down the columns.
- ® Column at the far left below indicates which sound is being practiced in each row of words.
- ® Dictate words for seven minutes, correcting errors when they occur.

<u>VCe</u>	spine	slide	vote	pride
<u>oo</u>	booth	coop	food	spoon
<u>wh</u>	white	whale	when	while
<u>oo</u>				
<u>ai</u>	pail	trail	paint	faint
<u>end blends</u>	milk	belt	crisp	duct
<u>end blends</u>	grand	rest	sent	limp
<u>sight</u>	there	were	where	they
<u>ow</u>				
<u>ai</u>	jail	main	grain	drain
<u>VCe</u>	crime	tube	slope	lake
<u>oo</u>				
<u>ow</u>	crow	glow	window	grown
<u>compound</u>	rainfall	timeline	airport	snapshot
<u>ow</u>				
<u>-ng/-nk</u>	thing	sank	hung	drink

- At each Session, dictate two of the following sentences.
- Learner repeats the sentence and writes it on paper.

We went for a ride on the subway.

Does Peg want to sing a song?

The wet dog ran from the bathroom.

Sunshine will help the grass grow green.

Set the chain on the chair.

Did you forget the popcorn?

Make a silk quilt for their bed.

I like some milk with a cupcake.

Their home is on the hillside.

Does Rick like hotdogs?

- Check for capitalization and punctuation.
- Learner reads aloud the sentences just written.

- Learner reads the list of words just written.

5 INTRODUCE NEW MATERIAL 5 MIN.

1. Introduce New Sound
- Show the Card and say the sound.
- Learner repeats the sound and traces it in the sand tray.

Card: **Sound Card 42**   ow   /ow/ as in owl

Rule: This is the second sound for <u>ow</u>. <u>ow</u> is the first choice for /ow/ (owl) at the end of a word or when /ow/ is followed by <u>n</u> or <u>l</u>.

- Learner reads corresponding words from the Word Book, page 90.

- Dictate the following words.
- Learner repeats each word, <u>Touch Spells</u> each word and says each sound out loud while writing the word on paper.

cow   now   plow   down   how   brown   frown   clown

- Learner reads the list of words just written.

® After teaching the sound, enter some of the words above in the blank spaces of ④ **SPELL WORDS.**

2. Introduce New Sound
- Show the Card and say the sound.
- Learner repeats the sound and traces it in the sand tray.

Card: **Sound Card 40**   oo   /oo/ as in book

Rule: This is the second sound for <u>oo</u>.

- Learner reads corresponding words from the Word Book, page 90.

- Dictate the following words.
- Learner repeats each word, <u>Touch Spells</u> each word and says each sound out loud while writing the word on paper.

book   stood   wood   look   cook   good   foot   shook

- Learner reads the list of words just written.

® After teaching the sound, enter some of the words above in the blank spaces of ④ **SPELL WORDS.**

CORRECTING SPELLING ERRORS

- Use questions to help Learner self correct when spelling errors are made.
  If <u>stood</u> is spelled <u>stud</u>, ask,
      "What is the vowel sound?"
      "How do you spell that sound?"

SONDAY SYSTEM 1 LEARNING PLAN

Reading Level 29

6 READ ALOUD

- Choose one of the following activities at each Session.

a) **Sentences, Word Book,** page 91.

b) **Read a Book.**
  - Sonday System® Readers, Level 29 a–c.
  - Focus on comprehension by asking factual and predictive questions. Predictive questions encourage the reader to predict future action or events from the text.

    Examples: What do you think he saw?
    How long will it take to build the wall?

c) **Reread Reading Strips** 26–28.

d) **Board Game.** Word Cards (gold).

HELPER'S NOTE

Tracing helps the Learner with reading. <u>Touch Spelling</u> helps the Learner with spelling.

Reading Level 30

MATERIALS NEEDED

- Watch Instructional Video • Sound Cards 1–44 • Blend Cards 1–29 • Sand Tray • Paper and pencil
- Word Cards (light blue, tan 1–3) • Sight Word Cards (red) 1–37 • Word Book • Reading Marker
- Reading Window and Strips 27–28 • Board Game • Book to read

1 READ SOUNDS

- Review Sound Cards **1–43** (every Session)

- Review Blend Cards **1–29** (every 3rd Session)

- Learner reads sound of each card aloud.
- Go through the cards rapidly. The goal is to have automatic responses.

REMINDER | Ask for two sounds of all single vowels, <u>ow</u>, <u>oo</u> and <u>y</u>.

2 SPELL SOUNDS

- Dictate the following sounds, one at a time.

oy   oo (as in book)   ow (as in owl)   all   ing   sl

- Learner repeats the sound.
- Learner writes the sound on paper or in the sand tray.

QUESTIONS TO ASK THE LEARNER
How would you write long /a/ in the middle of a word before <u>n</u> or <u>l</u>? (Answer: ai)
How do you write long /o/ at the end of a word? (Answer: ow)
What are four ways to spell long /a/? (Answer: ay, a–e, a, ai)
What are three ways of spelling long /e/? (Answer: ee, e–e, e)
How do you spell /k/ after a short vowel? (Answer: –ck)

SONDAY SYSTEM 1 LEARNING PLAN
Reading Level 30

③ READ WORDS

5 MIN.

Learner reads aloud from the following sources. Material is provided for several Sessions.

1. Word Book, page 92, Review VCe, Short Vowels.
2. Word Book, page 90, ow, oo.
3. Word Book, page 93, Review with ow, oo.
4. Word Book, page 94, Compound Words 2.
5. Word Book, Page 155, Level 30, Nonsense Words.

6. Sight Word Cards 1–37.
7. Word Cards (tan and gold mixed).
8. Word Book, page 134, Fluency practice, Level 30.
9. Word Book, review any previous pages.

④ SPELL WORDS

7 MIN.

- Dictate the following words to the Learner.
- Learner repeats each word, <u>Touch Spells</u> each word and says each sound out loud while writing the word on paper.
- Dictate each word aloud, reading down the columns.
- Column at the far left below indicates which sound is being practiced in each row of words.
- ® Dictate words for seven minutes, correcting errors when they occur.

<u>VCe</u>	time	bake	like	ride
<u>wh/-ck</u>	which	slick	whip	stuck
<u>-ing</u>		___	___	___
<u>er</u>		___	___	___
<u>oo</u>	hook	took	cook	good
<u>end blends</u>	melt	silk	lisp	pact
<u>ow</u>	how	plow	growl	frown
<u>end blends</u>	swift	damp	sift	trust
<u>-ing</u>		___	___	___
<u>sight</u>	your	done	gone	don't
<u>ai</u>	stain	pain	faint	brain
<u>VCe</u>	robe	hive	cube	shave
<u>ow</u>	snow	blow	shadow	blown
<u>-er</u>		___	___	___
<u>compound</u>	rainbow	daytime	windmill	caveman
<u>ow</u>	now	bow	crown	down

- Learner reads the list of words just written.

- At each Session, dictate two of the following sentences.
- Learner repeats the sentence and writes it on paper.

Now is the time to go home.

The clown was all in green.

The dog will howl at the moon.

Did you press the silk gown?

He took a chunk of cake.

Look at your left foot!

Can you cook a good lunch?

Bring the wood to the fire.

The wool vest will soon fit you.

Bait my hook so I can fish.

- Check for capitalization and punctuation.
- Learner reads aloud the sentences just written.

Reading Level 30

5 INTRODUCE NEW MATERIAL   5 MIN.

1. Introduce New Sound

- Show the Card and say the sound.
- Learner repeats the sound and traces it in the sand tray.

Card: **Sound Card 35 suffix** $\boxed{\text{-ing}}$ /ing/ as in falling

Rule: A suffix is added after a root or base word.

- Learner reads words from the Word Book, page 95.

- Dictate the following words.
- Learner repeats each word, <u>Touch Spells</u> each word and says each sound out loud while writing the word on paper.

| farming | looking | calling | picking | playing | resting |

- Learner reads the list of words just written.

® After teaching the sound, enter some of the words above in the blank spaces of ④ **SPELL WORDS.**

CORRECTING SPELLING ERRORS

- Use questions to help Learner self correct when spelling errors are made.
  When <u>sticking</u> is spelled as <u>stiking</u>, or <u>jumping</u> as <u>juping</u>, ask,
    "What is the word before you add /ing/?"
    "Write that base word. Now add the /ing/ and write it again."
- Learner rewrites the misspelled word so it is correctly spelled twice.

---

2. Introduce New Sound

- Show the Card and say the sound.
- Learner repeats the sound and traces it in the sand tray.

Card: **Sound Card 44** $\boxed{\text{er}}$ /er/ as in farmer

Rule: <u>er</u> is found in the middle of a word or at the end as a suffix.

- Learner reads words from the Word Book, page 96.

- Dictate the following words.
- Learner repeats each word, <u>Touch Spells</u> each word and says each sound out loud while writing the word on paper.

| her | perch | term | sooner | deeper | blacker |

- Learner reads the list of words just written.

® After teaching the sound, enter some of the words above in the blank spaces of ④ **SPELL WORDS.**

CORRECTING SPELLING ERRORS

- Use questions to help Learner self correct when spelling errors are made.
  When <u>blacker</u> is spelled as <u>blaker</u>, or <u>deeper</u> is spelled as <u>deper</u>, ask,
    "What was the word before you added /er/?"
    "Write that base word. Now add /er/ and write it again."
- Learner rewrites the misspelled word so it is correctly spelled twice.

SONDAY SYSTEM 1 LEARNING PLAN

Reading Level 30

6 READ ALOUD

• Choose one of the following activities at each Session.

a) Sentences, Word Book, page 97.

b) Read a Book.
- Sonday System® Readers, Level 30 a-c.
- See page 128 of the Word Book for a list of beginning reading books.

c) Repeated Reading.
From a book have the Learner read a text selection three times. Time each reading for one minute. With each repetition, the reader will read a few more words. Success and improvement are readily apparent. Rereading builds fluency.

d) Board Game. Word Cards (light blue).

e) Reread Reading Strips 27–28.

HELPER'S NOTE	Positive, encouraging comments renew enthusiasm.
CHECK FOR MASTERY	Use Mastery Check 30, on the following page, to check progress.

Mastery Check for Reading
Use after Level 30

Using the Sonday System 1 Learning Plan format, incorporate Mastery Check for Reading in the 3. Read Words section. Have the Learner read the words aloud. Time limit is 30 seconds. If fewer than 90% of the words are read accurately, teach two more sessions and give Form B during the 3. Read Words section of the third session. Alternate Forms A and B at every third session until the Learner reaches 90%.

HELPER'S NOTE Both Form A and B contain the same words but in a different order to avoid memorization of the sequence and require the Learner to read each word.

Have the student read the test from the Word Book, p. 147.

Reading Level 30 – Form A

former	crime	rocker	square
cookbook	faster	footprint	flower
want	been	any	their
stuffing	raining	sweeping	marching
paycheck	shower	rosebud	brown

Reading Level 30 – Form B

sweeping	marching	want	been
stuffing	brown	rosebud	raining
square	rocker	paycheck	shower
crime	footprint	flower	former
their	any	faster	cookbook

Count the number of words correctly read and multiply by 5 to obtain the percentage correct or use the Conversion Chart below.

CONVERSION CHART

# Correct	%	# Correct	%	# Correct	%
1	5%	8	40%	15	75%
2	10%	9	45%	16	80%
3	15%	10	50%	17	85%
4	20%	11	55%	18	90%
5	25%	12	60%	19	95%
6	30%	13	65%	20	100%
7	35%	14	70%		

The Learner should have 90% accuracy on the this test and 85% accuracy on the Spelling Mastery Check before moving to the next level.

Mastery Check for Spelling
Use after Level 30

Dictate the following words, reading down the columns. Repeat the words if necessary, but don't help the Learner make corrections. The goal is to determine what has been learned and how well the Learner can spell independently.

shape	clown	farmer	speech
drain	flashing	vote	crowd
blend	grasp	paint	any
shoot	pancake	left	dump
felt	stood	cute	shook

If 17 of the 20 words have been correctly spelled proceed to the next Level.

If four or more words are misspelled categorize the errors in the columns below by marking the letter or letters which represent the correct spelling. For example:

If	stood	is spelled as	stud	mark oo
If	paint	is spelled as	pant	mark ai
If	felt	is spelled as	fell	mark –lt
If	dump	is spelled as	dup	mark –mp

Errors	Word Book page	Errors	Word Book page	Errors	Word Book page
a ☐	2,3	s blends ☐	36	-nd ☐	74
e ☐	18	l blends ☐	39,40	-nt ☐	75
i ☐	4	r blends ☐	43,44	-mp ☐	75
o ☐	5	ink ☐	66	-ft ☐	76
u ☐	12	oo ☐	67,90	-lt ☐	85
ee ☐	15	VCe ☐	71	-lk ☐	85
sh ☐	24	ow ☐	79,90	-sp ☐	85
ch ☐	51	ai ☐	80	-ct ☐	85
all ☐	53	er ☐	96		
th ☐	56	any ☐	Sight Word		
ar ☐	62				

When you have identified the letters/sounds that need more practice, you may reuse Levels 28 – 30 or you may create Personalized Learning Plans following the instructions on the next two pages. The Word Book pages listed above will provide lists of words to use in creating learning plans. After at least four practice Sessions give this test again before moving to Level 31.

Creating A Personal Learning Plan

Using the form on the following page, construct a Personal Learning Plan to practice words and sounds that were missed in the Mastery Check along with words that have been mastered.

READ SOUNDS

- Use Sound Cards.
- Review all sounds that have been taught. Do this at every Session.

SPELL SOUNDS

- Use known sounds. Include those missed in the Mastery Check.
- Dictate 10 review sounds in 2 minutes or less at every Session.

READ WORDS

- Use Word Cards or Word Book lists that have been introduced.
- Read review words for 5 minutes at every Session.

SPELL WORDS

- Use words from the Word Cards or the Word Book that have been practiced. Include words that reinforce the sounds spelled incorrectly on the Mastery Check.
- Use sentences from the Word Book or create your own using words and sounds that have been taught.

READ ALOUD

- Use a Book to read, Reading Strips, or Board Game.

Learning Plan

① READ SOUNDS

- Review Sound Cards _____

② SPELL SOUNDS

___ ___ ___ ___ ___ ___ ___ ___ ___ ___ ___ ___ ___

③ READ WORDS

- Word Book page _____
- Word Cards _____

④ SPELL WORDS

1. _____ _____ _____ _____
2. _____ _____ _____ _____
3. _____ _____ _____ _____
4. _____ _____ _____ _____
5. _____ _____ _____ _____

- Dictate phrases or sentences
  1. _____
  2. _____

- Learner reads words and sentences just written.

⑤ READ ALOUD

Book to read

Reading Strip

Board Game

Reading Level 31

MATERIALS NEEDED

- Watch Instructional Video • Sound Cards 1–46 • Blend Cards 1–29 • Sand Tray • Paper and pencil
- Word Cards (tan 1–3, gold) • Sight Word Cards (red) 1–40 • Word Book • Reading Marker
- Reading Window and Strip 28 • Board Game • Book to read

1 READ SOUNDS

- Review Sound Cards **1–44** (every Session)

- Review Blend Cards **1–29** (every 3rd Session)

- Learner reads sound of each card aloud.
- Go through the cards rapidly. The goal is to have automatic responses.

REMINDER | Ask for two sounds of all single vowels, <u>ow</u>, <u>oo</u>, and <u>y</u>.

2 SPELL SOUNDS

- Dictate the following sounds, one at a time.

  th   **oo** (as in book)   **ow** (as in owl)   **ing**   **er**   **ar**   **gr**   **oo** (as in moon)

- Learner repeats the sound.
- Learner writes the sound on paper or in the sand tray.

QUESTIONS TO ASK THE LEARNER

How would you write long /a/ in the middle of a word before <u>n</u> or <u>l</u> ? (Answer: ai)
How do you write long /a/ at the end of a word? (Answer: ay)
How do you write long /o/ at the end of a word? (Answer: ow)

SONDAY SYSTEM 1 LEARNING PLAN
Reading Level 31

3 READ WORDS

5 MIN.

Learner reads aloud from the following sources. Material is provided for several Sessions.

1. Word Book, page 92, Review VCe, Short Vowels.
2. Word Book, page 95, –ing.
3. Word Book, page 96, er, –er.
4. Word Book, page 98, Review –ing, er, –er.
5. Word Book, page 94, Compound Words 2.
6. Sight Word Cards 1–37.
7. Word Cards (tan and gold mixed).
8. Word Book, review any previous pages.

4 SPELL WORDS

7 MIN.

- Dictate the following words to the Learner.
- Learner repeats each word, <u>Touch Spells</u> each word and says each sound out loud while writing the word on paper.
- Dictate each word aloud, reading down the columns.

<u>VCe</u>	life	file	mole	smile
<u>-ing</u>	telling	farming	milking	painting
<u>oo</u>	wood	stood	hook	brook
<u>ai</u>	drain	grain	wait	jail
<u>-tch</u>	___	___	___	
<u>sight</u>	gone	___	___	
<u>ow</u>	clown	brow	town	gown
<u>-er</u>	charter	corner	former	harder
<u>-dge</u>	___	___	___	
<u>sight</u>	where	there	some	come
<u>-ck/-ing</u>	sticking	packing	cracking	locking
<u>VCe</u>	bone	rave	stone	mule
<u>-tch</u>	___	___	___	
<u>ow/-ing</u>	showing	blowing	snowing	growing
<u>compound</u>	stingray	lipstick	somehow	anyway
<u>-er</u>	teller	farmer	cracker	darker
<u>-dge</u>	___	___	___	
<u>end blends</u>	lump	craft	slant	mask

- Learner reads the list of words just written.

- At each Session, dictate two of the following sentences.
- Learner repeats the sentence and writes it on paper.

Dave is picking ripe plums.

The boys are playing in the park.

Why are you looking for snails?

Are you showing me all of the flowers?

I will be calling you in the morning.

It was raining all day long.

It is harder to dig deep holes.

There is a dent in the bumper of the car.

Tim ran faster than the rest of the boys.

The farmer was planting the corn.

- Check for capitalization and punctuation.
- Learner reads aloud the sentences just written.

Reading Level 31

⑤ INTRODUCE NEW MATERIAL

1. Introduce New Sight Words
• Teach the following Sight Words, one in each Session.
• These words cannot be sounded out and need to be memorized.

Card: **Sight Word Cards 38–40** | have | | give | | live |

• Show the Learner one Sight Word Card, say it aloud and ask the Learner to repeat it.
• Learner traces the letters on the table while saying the letter names.
• Learner repeats the word before and after tracing.
• Learner writes new Sight Word on paper.
® After teaching, enter these words in the blank spaces of ④ **SPELL WORDS,** to dictate during the next Session.

2. Introduce New Sound
• Show the Card and say the sound.
• Learner repeats the sound and traces it in the sand tray.

Card: **Sound Card 45** | -tch | /ch/ as in match

Rule: Use –tch after a short vowel, usually at the end of a word. (The sound /ch/ is spelled ch when it follows anything except a short vowel, such as a consonant or a vowel pair. Examples: porch, bench, speech, coach.)

• Learner reads corresponding words from the Word Book, page 99.

• Dictate the following words.
• Learner repeats each word, Touch Spells each word and says each sound out loud while writing the word on paper.

catch   pitch   batch   match   clutch   itch

• Learner reads the list of words just written.
® After teaching the sound, enter some of the words above in the blank spaces of ④ **SPELL WORDS.**

CORRECTING SPELLING ERRORS

• Use questions to help Learner self correct when spelling errors are made.
    When pitch is spelled as pich, ask,
        "What is the last sound in that word?"
        "How do you write that after a short vowel?"
• Learner rewrites the misspelled word so it is correctly spelled twice.

SONDAY SYSTEM 1 LEARNING PLAN

Reading Level 31

INTRODUCE NEW MATERIAL

5 MIN.

3. Introduce New Sound

- Show the Card and say the sound.
- Learner repeats the sound and traces it in the sand tray.

Card: **Sound Card 46** | -dge | /j/ as in fudge

Rule: Use <u>–dge</u> after a short vowel, usually at the end of a word. (The sound /j/ is spelled <u>–ge</u> when it follows anything except a short vowel, such as a consonant, a vowel pair, or a long vowel. Examples: fringe, forge, gouge, page, rage.)

- Learner reads corresponding words from the Word Book, page 99.

- Dictate the following words.
- Learner repeats each word, <u>Touch Spells</u> each word and says each sound out loud while writing the word on paper.

| fudge | badge | lodge | bridge | wedge | judge |

- Learner reads the list of words just written.

® After teaching the sound, enter some of the words above in the blank spaces of ④ **SPELL WORDS**.

CORRECTING SPELLING ERRORS

- Use questions to help Learner self correct when spelling errors are made.
  When <u>fudge</u> is spelled as <u>fuge</u>, ask,
  "What is the last sound in that word?"
  "How do you write that after a short vowel?"
- Learner rewrites the misspelled word so it is correctly spelled twice.

READ ALOUD

10 MIN.

- Choose one of the following activities at each Session.

a) Sentences, Word Book, page 100.

b) Read a Book.
   - Sonday System® Readers, Level 31 a–c.
   - See page 128 of the Word Book for a list of beginning reading books. Reread.

c) Reading Strip 28.

d) Board Game. Word Cards (tan, gold).

HELPER'S NOTE

If the student is self conscious about tracing on the desk at school, suggest tracing on the leg under the desk.

Reading Level 32

MATERIALS NEEDED

- Watch Instructional Video • Sound Cards 1–49 • Blend Cards 1–29 • Sand Tray • Paper and pencil
- Transparency and Washable Pen • Word Cards (light blue, tan 1–3, gold) • Sight Word Cards (red) 1–40
- Word Book • Reading Marker • Board Game • Book to read

---

1 ## READ SOUNDS

- Review Sound Cards **1–46** (every Session)

- Review Blend Cards **1–29** (every 3rd Session)

- Learner reads sound of each card aloud.
- Go through the cards rapidly. The goal is to have automatic responses.

REMINDER | Drill builds fast recognition.

2 ## SPELL SOUNDS

- Dictate the following sounds, one at a time.

    er   e   -mp   ing   or

- Learner repeats the sound.
- Learner writes the sound on paper or in the sand tray.

QUESTIONS TO ASK THE LEARNER

How do you write long /o/ at the end of a word? (Answer: ow)
How do you write /ch/ after a short vowel? (Answer: –tch)
How else can you write /ch/? (Answer: ch)
How do you write /j/ after a short vowel? (Answer: –dge)
How many ways can you spell long /a/? (Answer: a, ay, ai, a-e)

SONDAY SYSTEM 1 LEARNING PLAN

Reading Level 32

 ## 3 READ WORDS

 5 MIN.

Learner reads aloud from the following sources. Material is provided for several Sessions.

1. Word Book, page 98, Review -ing, er, -er.
2. Word Book, page 99, -tch, -dge.
3. Word Book, page 101, Review with -tch, -dge.
4. Word Book, page 102, Review with -tch, ch.

5. Word Book, page 103, Worksheet with -ch, -tch.
6. Sight Word Cards (red) 1–40.
7. Word Book, review any previous pages.

4 SPELL WORDS

 7 MIN.

- Dictate the following words to the Learner.
- Learner repeats each word, <u>Touch Spells</u> each word and says each sound out loud while writing the word on paper.
- Dictate each word aloud, reading down the columns.
- ® Dictate words for seven minutes, correcting errors when they occur

<u>VCe</u>	slope	mute	grave	froze
<u>-tch</u>	hatch	snitch	clutch	crutch
<u>aw</u>		____	____	____
<u>oi</u>		____	____	____
<u>oo/oo</u>	smooth	crook	booth	took
<u>ow/ow</u>	flow	frown	showing	down
<u>-dge</u>	bridge	fudge	pledge	judge
<u>-er</u>	locker	clicker	border	smarter
<u>oa</u>		____	____	____
<u>sight</u>	any	want	says	been
<u>-tch</u>	ditch	pitch	itch	notch
<u>aw</u>		____	____	____
<u>VCe</u>	smile	prime	slime	gripe
<u>-ing</u>	marking	looking	fishing	sinking
<u>compound</u>	mailbox	raindrop	wishbone	windmill
<u>oi</u>		____	____	____
<u>-dge</u>	edge	lodge	ridge	hedge
<u>end blends</u>	standing	resting	wilt	lisp
<u>oa</u>		____	____	____

- Learner reads the list of words just written.

- At each Session, dictate two of the following sentences.
- Learner repeats the sentence and writes it on paper.

Were you on time to catch the train?

Pitch the ball to home base.

A stitch in time saves nine.

Hitch up and ride into the sunset.

He can cross the bridge on his bike.

Have you made a batch of fudge?

Try to match the paint for that patch.

We will soon have time to play dodge ball.

Did you say the pledge to the flag?

The judge will steer his car into the driveway.

- Check for capitalization and punctuation.
- Learner reads aloud the sentences just written.

Reading Level 32

5 INTRODUCE NEW MATERIAL

5 MIN.

1. Introduce New Sound
- Show the Card and say the sound.
- Learner repeats the sound and traces it in the sand tray.

Card: **Sound Card 47** | aw | /aw/ as in saw

Rule: <u>aw</u> is usually at the end of a word or followed by <u>n</u> or <u>l</u>.

- Learner reads words from the Word Book, page 104.

- Dictate the following words.
- Learner repeats each word, <u>Touch Spells</u> each word and says each sound out loud while writing the word on paper.

| saw | draw | law | jaw | paw | lawn |

- Learner reads the list of words just written.

® After teaching the sound, enter some of the words above in the blank spaces of ④ **SPELL WORDS.**

2. Introduce New Sound
- Show the Card and say the sound.
- Learner repeats the sound and traces it in the sand tray.

Card: **Sound Card 48** | oa | /oa/ as in coat

Rule: <u>oa</u> makes the sound of long <u>o</u> and comes at the beginning or middle of short words.

- Learner reads words from the Word Book, page 105.

- Dictate the following words.
- Learner repeats each word, <u>Touch Spells</u> each word and says each sound out loud while writing the word on paper.

| coat | toast | load | road | soap | goal |

- Learner reads the list of words just written.

® After teaching the sound, enter some of the words above in the blank spaces of ④ **SPELL WORDS.**

CORRECTING SPELLING ERRORS

- Use questions to help Learner self correct when spelling errors are made.
  When <u>soap</u> is spelled as <u>sope</u>, ask,
    "What is the vowel sound in that word?"
    "How else can you write long /o/ in the middle of short words?"
- Learner rewrites the misspelled word so it is correctly spelled twice.

SONDAY SYSTEM 1 LEARNING PLAN

Reading Level 32

INTRODUCE NEW MATERIAL

3. Introduce New Sound
- Show the Card and say the sound.
- Learner repeats the sound and traces it in the sand tray.

Card: **Sound Card 49** /oi/ as in coin

Rule: <u>oi</u> comes at the beginning or in the middle of a word. (<u>oy</u> makes the same sound at the end of a word.)

- Learner reads words from the Word Book, page 104.

- Dictate the following words.
- Learner repeats each word, <u>Touch Spells</u> each word and says each sound out loud while writing the word on paper.

| coin | boil | spoil | moist | coil | join |

- Learner reads the list of words just written.
- ® After teaching the sound, enter some of the words above in the blank spaces of ④ **SPELL WORDS.**

CORRECTING SPELLING ERRORS

- Use questions to help Learner self correct when spelling errors are made.
  When <u>broil</u> is spelled as <u>broyl</u>, ask,
  "What is the vowel sound in that word?"
  "How do you write that sound in the middle of a word?"
- Learner rewrites the misspelled word so it is correctly spelled twice.

READ ALOUD

- Choose one of the following activities at each Session.

a) Sentences, Word Book, page 106–107.

b) Read a Book.
  - Sonday System® Readers, Level 32 a–c.
  - Focus on comprehension by asking factual and predictive and inferential questions. Inferential questions encourage the reader to conclude or deduce the answer based on evidence from the text.
    Examples: How would you have solved that problem?
                  What was your favorite part of the story?

c) Board Game. Word Cards (tan, gold, mixed).

HELPER'S NOTE

When involved in a compelling book, let the reader continue reading beyond the suggested time.

Reading Level 33

MATERIALS NEEDED

- Watch Instructional Video • Sound Cards 1–49 • Blend Cards 1–29 • Sand Tray • Paper and pencil
- Word Cards (light blue) • Sight Word Cards (red) 1–44 • Word Book • Reading Marker • Book to read

1 READ SOUNDS

- Review Sound Cards **1–49** (every Session)

- Review Blend Cards **1–29** (every 3rd Session)

- Learner reads sound of each card aloud.
- Go through the cards rapidly. The goal is to have automatic responses.

REMINDER | Ask for two sounds of <u>a</u>, <u>e</u>, <u>i</u>, <u>o</u>, <u>u</u>, <u>ow</u>, <u>oo</u>, and <u>y</u>.

2 SPELL SOUNDS

- Dictate the following sounds, one at a time.

ch   oo (as in book)   ow (as in owl)   aw

- Learner repeats the sound.
- Learner writes the sound on paper or in the sand tray.

QUESTIONS TO ASK THE LEARNER

How do you write long /o/ four ways? (Answer: o, o-e, ow, oa)
How do you write /ch/ after a short vowel? (Answer: -tch)
How else can you write /ch/? (Answer: ch)
What are four ways to spell long /a/? (Answer: a, ay, ai, a-e)
What are two ways to spell /oi/? (Answer: oi, oy)
Spell /w/ two ways? (Answer: w, wh)

SONDAY SYSTEM 1 LEARNING PLAN

Reading Level 33

READ WORDS

5 MIN.

Learner reads aloud from the following sources. Material is provided for several Sessions.

1. Word Book, page 105, oa.
2. Word Book, page 104, aw, oi.
3. Word Book, page 108, Review aw, oa, oi.
4. Word Book, page 101, Review with -tch, -dge.
5. Word Book, page 98, Review -ing, er, -er.
6. Sight Word Cards (red) 1–40.
7. Word Cards (light blue).
8. Word Book, page 135, Fluency practice, Level 33.

SPELL WORDS

7 MIN.

• Dictate the following words to the Learner.
• Learner repeats each word, <u>Touch Spells</u> each word and says each sound out loud while writing the word on paper.
• Dictate each word aloud, reading down the columns.

VCe	time	bite	line	grape
aw	raw	claw	thaw	draw
oo/oo	boost	hood	food	stood
soft c		___	___	___
sight	want		___	___
ow/ow	growing	gown	snowing	town
oa	soap	float	boat	toast
soft g		___	___	___
sight	have	give	live	anyone
oi	coin	coil	spoil	moist
-tch	hitch	ditch	batch	stitch
soft c		___	___	___
VCe	slave	spine	slope	rope
oa	road	coat	coast	foam
aw	law	lawn	drawn	yawn
soft g		___	___	___
-dge	wedge	ledge	badge	trudge
oi	join	point	foil	broil

• Learner reads the list of words just written.

• At each Session, dictate two of the following sentences.
• Learner repeats the sentence and writes it on paper.

Do you have to mow the lawn?

The sun comes up at dawn.

The moist, black soil is good for planting.

Broil the fish and give it to me.

I saw three big coins deep in the pool.

Can you kick the ball past the goal?

Point to the fox with the gray claws.

I saw you yawning in class today.

The soap made foam in the bathtub.

A toad and a goat were sleeping in the grass.

• Check for capitalization and punctuation.
• Learner reads aloud the sentences just written.

Reading Level 33

INTRODUCE NEW MATERIAL

5

1. Introduce New Sight Words
• Teach the following Sight Words, one in each Session.
• These words cannot be sounded out and need to be memorized.

Card: **Sight Word Cards 41-44**   could   would   should   very

• Show the Learner one Sight Word Card, say it aloud and ask the Learner to repeat it.
• Learner traces the letters on the table while saying the letter names.
• Learner repeats the word before and after tracing.
• Learner writes new Sight Word on paper.
® After teaching, enter these words in the blank spaces of ④ **SPELL WORDS,** to dictate during the next Session.

2. Introduce New Sound
• Show the Card and say the sound.
• Learner repeats the sound and traces it in the sand tray.

Card: **Sound Card 14**   c   /s/ as in ice.

Rule: <u>c</u> has the soft sound /s/ when followed by <u>e</u>, <u>i</u>, <u>y</u>.

• Learner reads words from the Word Book, page 109.

• Dictate the following words.
• Learner repeats each word, <u>Touch Spells</u> each word and says each sound out loud while writing the word on paper.

ice   dance   face   nice   place   mice

• Learner reads the list of words just written.
® After teaching the sound, enter some of the words above in the blank spaces of ④ **SPELL WORDS.**

CORRECTING SPELLING ERRORS

• Use questions to help Learner self correct when spelling errors are made.
   When <u>dance</u> is spelled as <u>dans</u> or <u>race</u> is spelled as <u>rase</u>, ask,
      "What is the last sound in that word?"
      "How else can you write that sound?"
• Learner rewrites the misspelled word so it is correctly spelled twice.

SONDAY SYSTEM 1 LEARNING PLAN

INTRODUCE NEW MATERIAL

3. Introduce New Sound

• Show the Card and say the sound.

• Learner repeats the sound and traces it in the sand tray.

Card: **Sound Card 15** g /j/ as in age.

Rule: g has the soft sound /j/ when g is followed by e, i, y.

• Learner reads words from the Word Book, page 109.

• Dictate the following words.

• Learner repeats each word, Touch Spells each word and says each sound out loud while writing the word on paper.

age   cage   plunge   page   large   hinge

• Learner reads the list of words just written.

® After teaching the sound, enter some of the words above in the blank spaces of ④ **SPELL WORDS.**

CORRECTING SPELLING ERRORS

• Use questions to help Learner self correct when spelling errors are made.
    When stage is spelled as stag or large is spelled as larg, ask,
        "What is the last sound in that word?"
        "How do you write that sound at the end of a word?"
• Learner rewrites the misspelled word so it is correctly spelled twice.

READ ALOUD

• Choose one of the following activities at each Session.

a) Sentences, Word Book, page 110.

b) Read a Book.
    – Sonday System® Readers, Level 33 a-c.
    – See page 128 of the Word Book for a list of beginning reading books.

c) Repeated Reading.
    From a book have the Learner read a text selection three times. Time each reading for one minute. With each repetition, the reader will read a few more words. Success and improvement are readily apparent. Rereading builds fluency.

d) Board Game. Sight Word Cards (red) 1-44.

HELPER'S NOTE

Encourage the Learner to read street signs, billboards, ads, video titles, and other words in the environment.

Mastery Check for Reading
Use after Level 33

Using the Sonday System 1 Learning Plan format, incorporate Mastery Check for Reading in the 3. Read Words section. Have the Learner read the words aloud. Time limit is 30 seconds. If fewer than 90% of the words are read accurately, teach two more sessions and give Form B during the 3. Read Words section of the third session. Alternate Forms A and B at every third session until the Learner reaches 90%.

HELPER'S NOTE — Both Form A and B contain the same words but in a different order to avoid memorization of the sequence and require the Learner to read each word.

<u>Have the student read the test from the Word Book, p. 148.</u>

Reading Level 33 – Form A

bench	could	stitch	very
trace	cell	voice	center
jawbone	charcoal	drawing	cardboard
germ	cube	gem	quake
pointer	plunge	broiler	wage

Reading Level 33 – Form B

charcoal	voice	center	jawbone
cell	trace	very	stitch
could	bench	broiler	wage
gem	plunge	pointer	quake
drawing	cube	germ	cardboard

Count the number of words correctly read and multiply by 5 to obtain the percentage correct or use the Conversion Chart below.

CONVERSION CHART

# Correct	%	# Correct	%	# Correct	%
1	5%	8	40%	15	75%
2	10%	9	45%	16	80%
3	15%	10	50%	17	85%
4	20%	11	55%	18	90%
5	25%	12	60%	19	95%
6	30%	13	65%	20	100%
7	35%	14	70%		

The Learner should have 90% accuracy on the this test and 85% accuracy on the Spelling Mastery Check before moving to the next level.

Mastery Check for Spelling
Use after Level 33

Dictate the following words, reading down the columns. Repeat the words if necessary, but don't help the Learner make corrections. The goal is to determine what has been learned and how well the Learner can spell independently.

draw	float	spoil	milk
pitch	edge	notch	budge
belt	lisp	act	should
very	have	barge	cube
smile	place	shorter	parking

If 17 of the 20 words have been correctly spelled proceed to the next Level.

If four or more words are misspelled categorize the errors in the columns below by marking the letter or letters which represent the correct spelling. For example:

If	pitch	is spelled as	pick	mark	-tch
If	draw	is spelled as	drau	mark	aw
If	edge	is spelled as	ege	mark	-dge
If	float	is spelled as	flote	mark	oa

Errors	Word Book page	Errors	Word Book page	Errors	Word Book page
a ☐	2,3	s blends ☐	36	-dge ☐	99
e ☐	18	l blends ☐	39,40	aw ☐	104
i ☐	4	r blends ☐	43,44	oi ☐	104
o ☐	5	VCe ☐	71	oa ☐	105
u ☐	12	-lt ☐	85	soft c ☐	109
sh ☐	24	-lk ☐	85	soft g ☐	109
-ck ☐	31	-sp ☐	85	have ☐	Sight Word
or ☐	53	-ct ☐	85	should ☐	Sight Word
ing ☐	95	er ☐	96	very ☐	Sight Word
ar ☐	62	-tch ☐	99		

When you have identified the letters/sounds that need more practice, you may reuse Levels 31 – 33 or you may create Personalized Learning Plans following the instructions on the next two pages. The Word Book pages listed above will provide lists of words to use in creating learning plans. After at least four practice Sessions give this test again.

Using the form on the following page, construct a Personal Learning Plan to practice words and sounds that were missed in the Mastery Check along with words that have been mastered.

1 READ SOUNDS

- Use Sound Cards.
- Review all sounds that have been taught. Do this at every Session.

2 SPELL SOUNDS

- Use known sounds. Include those missed in the Mastery Check.
- Dictate 10 review sounds in 2 minutes or less at every Session.

3 READ WORDS

- Use Word Cards or Word Book lists that have been introduced.
- Read review words for 5 minutes at every Session.

4 SPELL WORDS

- Use words from the Word Cards or the Word Book that have been practiced. Include words that reinforce the sounds spelled incorrectly on the Mastery Check.
- Use sentences from the Word Book or create your own using words and sounds that have been taught.

5 READ ALOUD

- Use a Book to read, Reading Strips, or Board Game.

Learning Plan

1 READ SOUNDS

- Review Sound Cards _____

2 SPELL SOUNDS

___ ___ ___ ___ ___ ___ ___ ___ ___ ___ ___ ___ ___

3 READ WORDS

- Word Book page _____
- Word Cards _____

4 SPELL WORDS

1. _____ _____ _____ _____ _____
2. _____ _____ _____ _____ _____
3. _____ _____ _____ _____ _____
4. _____ _____ _____ _____ _____
5. _____ _____ _____ _____ _____

- Dictate phrases or sentences
  1. _____
  2. _____
- Learner reads words and sentences just written.

5 READ ALOUD

Book to read

Reading Strip

Board Game

SONDAY SYSTEM 1 LEARNING PLAN

Reading Level 34

MATERIALS NEEDED

- Watch Instructional Video • Sound Cards 1–52 • Blend Cards 1–29 • Sand Tray • Paper and pencil • Transparency and Washable Pen
- Word Cards (tan 1–3, gold, orange) • Sight Word Cards (red) 1–44 • Word Book • Reading Marker • Book to read

---

1 READ SOUNDS

 2 MIN.

- Review Sound Cards **1–49** (every Session)

- Review Blend Cards **1–29** (every 3rd Session)

- Learner reads sound of each card aloud.
- Go through the cards rapidly. The goal is to have automatic responses.

REMINDER | Practice reinforces learning.

---

2 SPELL SOUNDS

 2 MIN.

- Dictate the following sounds, one at a time.

    ow (as in owl)   **aw**

- Learner repeats the sound.
- Learner writes the sound on paper or in the sand tray.

QUESTIONS TO ASK THE LEARNER

How do you write long /o/ at the end of a word? (Answer: ow)
How do you write long /o/ in the middle of a word? (Answer: oa)
How do you write /ch/ after a short vowel? (Answer: –tch)
How do you write /j/ after a short vowel? (Answer: –dge)
What are the two ways to write /s/? (Answer: s, c)
What are the three ways to write /j/? (Answer: j, g, –dge)

SONDAY SYSTEM 1 LEARNING PLAN
Reading Level 34

3 READ WORDS

5 MIN.

Learner reads aloud from the following sources. Material is provided for several Sessions.

1. Word Book, page 101, Review with –tch, –dge.
2. Word Book, page 109, Soft c and Soft g.
3. Word Book, page 108, Review aw, oa, oi.
4. Word Book, page 111, Review Soft c and Soft g.

5. Word Book, page 84, Compound Words 1.
6. Word Book, page 112, Worksheet with –ge, –dge.
7. Sight Word Cards 1–44.
8. Word Book, review any previous pages.

4 SPELL WORDS

7 MIN.

- Dictate the following words to the Learner.
- Learner repeats each word, <u>Touch Spells</u> each word and says each sound out loud while writing the word on paper.
- Dictate each word aloud, reading down the columns.
- ® Dictate words for seven minutes, correcting errors when they occur.

<u>VCe</u>	life	tire	hire	while
<u>aw</u>	flaw	jaw	lawn	yawn
<u>oo/oo</u>	coop	wood	scoop	cook
<u>ea</u>	___	___	___	___
<u>ow/ow</u>	snow	crown	throw	frown
<u>soft c</u>	race	face	spice	rice
<u>ew</u>	___	___	___	___
<u>sight</u>	could	would	should	very
<u>soft c-g</u>	dance	large	prince	barge
<u>ear</u>	___	___	___	___
<u>-tch</u>	crutch	stitch	match	hatch
<u>VCe</u>	grove	cube	robe	mule
<u>soft g</u>	page	stage	fringe	plunge
<u>oa</u>	toad	goat	soak	coach
<u>ew</u>	___	___	___	___
<u>-dge</u>	judge	pledge	lodge	dodge
<u>oi</u>	coin	join	moist	spoil

- Learner reads the list of words just written.

- At each Session, dictate two of the following sentences.
- Learner repeats the sentence and writes it on paper.

The prince should ask her to dance twice.

Go to the place where the boat is floating.

Stand by the fence and look at the race.

Place the white mice back in the cage.

I like the fringe on your vest.

There is a very huge gem in the ring.

Bruce could plunge into the water.

Grace got on the stage to dance.

Would Mitch fix the hinge?

Can you trace a line at the edge?

- Check for capitalization and punctuation.
- Learner reads aloud the sentences just written.

Reading Level 34

INTRODUCE NEW MATERIAL   5 MIN.

1. Introduce New Sound
- Show the Card and say the sound.
- Learner repeats the sound and traces it in the sand tray.

Card: Sound Card 50 | ea | /ee/ as in team.

Rule: ea sounds like long /e/ and there is no sound difference or rule to distinguish it from ee. (Do not use ee for spelling words while establishing ea.)

- Learner reads words from the Word Book, page 113.

- Dictate the following words.
- Learner repeats each word, <u>Touch Spells</u> each word and says each sound out loud while writing the word on paper.

| cream | read | eat | seat | reach | team |

- Learner reads the list of words just written.
- ® After teaching the sound, enter some of the words above in the blank spaces of ④ **SPELL WORDS.**

CORRECTING SPELLING ERRORS

- Use questions to help Learner self correct when spelling errors are made.
  When <u>peach</u> is spelled as <u>peech</u> or <u>cream</u> is spelled as <u>creem</u>, ask,
      "What is the vowel sound in that word?"
      "How else can you write that sound in the middle of a word?"
- Learner rewrites the misspelled word so it is correctly spelled twice.

---

2. Introduce New Sound
- Show the Card and say the sound.
- Learner repeats the sound and traces it in the sand tray.

Card: Sound Card 51 | ew | /oo/ as in dew

Rule: ew is the first choice for writing /oo/ at the end of a word.

- Learner reads words from the Word Book, page 114.

- Dictate the following words.
- Learner repeats each word, <u>Touch Spells</u> each word and says each sound out loud while writing the word on paper.

| new | chew | blew | grew | flew | stew | dew |

- Learner reads the list of words just written.
- ® After teaching the sound, enter some of the words above in the blank spaces of ④ **SPELL WORDS.**

CORRECTING SPELLING ERRORS

- Use questions to help Learner self correct when spelling errors are made.
  When <u>grew</u> is spelled as <u>groo</u>, ask,
      "What is the last sound in that word?"
      "How do you write that sound at the end of a word?"
      "Where would you use <u>oo</u> in spelling a word?"

SONDAY SYSTEM 1 LEARNING PLAN

Reading Level 34

INTRODUCE NEW MATERIAL

3. Introduce New Sound
• Show the Card and say the sound.
• Learner repeats the sound and traces it in the sand tray.

Card: **Sound Card 52** | ear | /ear/ as in ear.

• Learner reads words from the Word Book, page 114.

• Dictate the following words.
• Learner repeats each word, <u>Touch Spells</u> each word and says each sound out loud while writing the word on paper.

hear   fear   near   dear   clear   spear

• Learner reads the list of words just written.
® After teaching the sound, enter some of the words above in the blank spaces of ④ **SPELL WORDS.**

READ ALOUD

• Choose one of the following activities at each Session.

a) Sentences, Word Book, page 115–116.

b) Read a Book.
- Sonday System® Readers, Level 34 a–c.
- See page 128 of the Word Book for a list of beginning reading books.

c) Board Game. Word Cards (tan 1–3, gold and orange, mixed) 1–44.

| HELPER'S NOTE | When the Learner can quickly explain the rule or reason for an correct response, the Learner has mastered that piece. |

Reading Level 35

MATERIALS NEEDED

- Watch Instructional Video • Sound Cards 1–54 • Blend Cards 1–29 • Sand Tray • Paper and pencil
- Word Cards (light blue) • Sight Word Cards (red) 1–44 • Word Book • Reading Marker • Book to read

1 READ SOUNDS

- Review Sound Cards **1–52** (every Session)

- Review Blend Cards **1–29** (every 3rd Session)

- Learner reads sound of each card aloud.
- Go through the cards rapidly. The goal is to have automatic responses.

REMINDER Ask for two sounds of <u>a</u>, <u>e</u>, <u>i</u>, <u>o</u>, <u>u</u>, <u>ow</u>, <u>oo</u>, <u>y</u>, <u>c</u> and g.

2 SPELL SOUNDS

- Dictate the following sounds, one at a time.

   ear   **ow** (as in owl)

- Learner repeats the sound.
- Learner writes the sound on paper or in the sand tray.

QUESTIONS TO ASK THE LEARNER

What are two ways to spell /oo/? (Answer: oo, ew)
How many ways can you write long /e/? (Answer: e, ee, e-e, ea)
How do your write long /o/ at the end of a word? (Answer: ow)
How do you write /ch/ after a short vowel? (Answer: –tch)
How do you write /j/ after a short vowel? (Answer: –dge)
What are two ways to write /s/? (Answer: s, c)
What are three ways of writing /j/? (Answer: j, g, –dge)
What are three ways of spelling long /i/? (Answer: i, y, i–e)

SONDAY SYSTEM 1 LEARNING PLAN
Reading Level 35

③ READ WORDS

5 MIN.

Learner reads aloud from the following sources. Material is provided for several Sessions.

1. Word Book, page 113, ea.
2. Word Book, page 114, ear, ew.
3. Word Book, page 117, Review with ea, ew, ear.
4. Word Book, page 108, Review aw, oa, oi.
5. Word Book, page 94, Compound Words 2.
6. Word Book, page 111, Review Soft c and Soft g.
7. Sight Word Cards 1–44.
8. Word Book, review any previous pages.

④ SPELL WORDS

7 MIN.

- Dictate the following words to the Learner.
- Learner repeats each word, <u>Touch Spells</u> each word and says each sound out loud while writing the word on paper.
- Dictate each word aloud, reading down the columns.

<u>VCe</u>	rice	mine	spice	flame
<u>igh</u>		———	———	———
<u>aw/ow</u>	draw	grow	claw	town
<u>ea</u>	team	teach	meal	lead
<u>ew</u>	new	stew	grew	blew
<u>ou</u>		———	———	———
<u>soft c</u>	lace	nice	space	price
<u>sight</u>	what	who	one	does
<u>ea</u>	speak	reach	cheap	heal
<u>-tch</u>	pitch	crutch	ditch	clutch
<u>igh</u>		———	———	———
<u>VCe</u>	slide	spine	make	take
<u>soft g</u>	wage	forge	cage	barge
<u>ear</u>	near	fear	clear	gear
<u>oa/oi</u>	load	point	soap	tinfoil
<u>-dge</u>	ridge	badge	hedge	nudge
<u>ou</u>		———	———	———
<u>ew</u>	chew	drew	flew	few

- At each Session, dictate two of the following sentences.
- Learner repeats the sentence and writes it on paper.

He ate fish and chips at the noon meal.

Would you clean your room and make it neat?

That brave team will reach the North Pole.

I can read it in the late news.

The cook put lean meat in the stew.

Dream on!

A new crew flew the airplane.

Liz threw the ball to her teammate.

Give me a few good men for the job.

Don't smear the fresh paint.

- Check for capitalization and punctuation.
- Learner reads aloud the sentences just written.

INTRODUCE NEW MATERIAL

5 MIN.

1. Introduce New Sound

- Show the Card and say the sound.
- Learner repeats the sound and traces it in the sand tray.

Card: **Sound Card 53** | igh | long /i/ as in night.

Rule: igh is usually at the end of a word or followed by t.

- Learner reads words from the Word Book, page 118.

- Dictate the following words.
- Learner repeats each word, Touch Spells each word and says each sound out loud while writing the word on paper.

| high | fight | sigh | right | bright | sight |

- Learner reads the list of words just written.

® After teaching the sound, enter some of the words above in the blank spaces of ④ **SPELL WORDS.**

CORRECTING SPELLING ERRORS

- Use questions to help Learner self correct when spelling errors are made.
    When bright is spelled as brite or light is spelled as lite, ask,
        "What is the vowel sound in that word?"
        "How do you usually write long /i/ before a t?"
- Learner rewrites the misspelled word so it is correctly spelled twice.

2. Introduce New Sound

- Show the Card and say the sound.
- Learner repeats the sound and traces it in the sand tray.

Card: **Sound Card 54** | ou | /ou/ as in mouth.

Rule: ou is the first choice for /ow/ in the middle of a word.

- Learner reads words from the Word Book, page 118.

- Dictate the following words.
- Learner repeats each word, Touch Spells each word and says each sound out loud while writing the word on paper.

| count | shout | proud | found | mouth | ounce |

- Learner reads the list of words just written.

® After teaching the sound, enter some of the words above in the blank spaces of ④ **SPELL WORDS.**

CORRECTING SPELLING ERRORS

- Use questions to help Learner self correct when spelling errors are made.
    When found is spelled as fownd, ask,
        "What is the vowel sound in that word?"
        "How do you write that sound in the middle of a word?"
        "How would you spell that sound at the end of a word?"

SONDAY SYSTEM 1 LEARNING PLAN

Reading Level 35

6 READ ALOUD

- Choose one of the following activities at each Session.

a) Sentences, Word Book, page 119.

b) Read a Book.
   - Sonday System® Readers, Level 35–36 a.
   - Focus on comprehension by asking factual and predictive and inferential questions. Inferential questions encourage the reader to conclude or deduce the answer based on evidence from the text.

   Examples: How would you have solved that problem?
                What was your favorite part of the story?

c) Board Game. Word Cards (light blue).

| HELPER'S NOTE | Fluent reading is a necessary forerunner to comprehension and school success. |

Reading Level 36

MATERIALS NEEDED

- Watch Instructional Video • Sound Cards 1–54 • Blend Cards 1–29 • Sand Tray • Paper and pencil
- Word Cards (light blue, tan 1-3, gold) • Sight Word Cards (red) 1–44 • Word Book • Reading Marker • Book to read

1 READ SOUNDS

- Review Sound Cards **1–54** (every Session)

- Review Blend Cards **1–29** (every 3rd Session)

- Learner reads sound of each card aloud.
- Go through the cards rapidly. The goal is to have automatic responses.

REMINDER | Mix the Sound Cards

2 SPELL SOUNDS

- Dictate the following sounds, one at a time.

  sp   -lt   gr

- Learner repeats the sound.
- Learner writes the sound on paper or in the sand tray.

QUESTIONS TO ASK THE LEARNER

What are two ways to spell /ow/ (as in owl)? (Answer: ow, ou)
What are two ways to spell /oo/? (Answer: oo, ew)
What are four ways to spell long /a/? (Answer: a, ay, ai, a-e)
What are two ways to spell /s/? (Answer: s, c)
What are four ways to spell long /e/? (Answer: e, ee, e-e, ea)
What are four ways to spell long /i/? (Answer: i, y, i-e, igh)
What are two ways to spell /ch/? (Answer: ch, -tch)

SONDAY SYSTEM 1 LEARNING PLAN
Reading Level 36

3 ## READ WORDS

Learner reads aloud from the following sources. Material is provided for several Sessions.

1. Word Book, page 118, igh, ou.
2. Word Cards (tan and gold mixed).
3. Word Book, page 120, Review igh, ou.
4. Word Book, page 117, Review with ea, ew, ear.

5. Sight Word Cards (red) 1–44.
6. Word Book, page 135, Fluency practice, Level 36.
7. Word Book, review any previous pages.

4 ## SPELL WORDS

- Dictate the following words to the Learner.
- Learner repeats each word, <u>Touch Spells</u> each word and says each sound out loud while writing the word on paper.
- Dictate each word aloud, reading down the columns.
- ® Dictate words for seven minutes, correcting errors when they occur

<u>ou</u>	found	mouth	spout	ground
<u>VCe</u>	drive	pride	gripe	slope
<u>igh</u>	light	bright	fight	slight
<u>ea</u>	lead	meal	reach	steam
<u>sight</u>	some	could	give	very
<u>ew</u>	grew	blew	stew	chew
<u>ou</u>	south	loud	proud	sound
<u>VCe</u>	shade	grade	stone	cute
<u>igh</u>	high	flight	fright	night
<u>ear</u>	near	fear	hear	clear
<u>soft c</u>	nice	dance	trace	since
<u>oa/oi</u>	roast	coin	coal	point
<u>-tch/ch</u>	hatch	pinch	stitch	porch
<u>soft g</u>	stage	germ	rage	fringe
<u>ai/ay</u>	drain	staying	claim	player
<u>-dge/-ge</u>	judge	forge	bridge	large
<u>aw/ow</u>	thaw	clown	yawn	crowd

- Learner reads the list of words just written.

- At each Session, dictate two of the following sentences.
- Learner repeats the sentence and writes it on paper.

Can you count the fish on the dock?

That is a sight to see.

I do not hear a sound.

The next flight is quite late.

He was proud of his new bike.

Do not bounce on the bed.

They will eat a pound of meat.

I think there is a mouse in the house.

I might speak to their teacher.

The ground was wet.

- Check for capitalization and punctuation.
- Learner reads aloud the sentences just written.

Reading Level 36

5 READ ALOUD

- Choose one of the following activities at each Session.

a) Sentences, Word Book, page 121.

b) Read a Book.
- Sonday System® Readers, Level 35–36 a–c.
- See page 128 of the Word Book for a list of beginning reading books.

c) Repeated Reading.
From a book have the Learner read a text selection three times. Time each reading for one minute. With each repetition, the reader will read a few more words. Success and improvement are readily apparent. Rereading builds fluency.

d) Board Game. Word Cards (light blue, tan 1–3, gold).

HELPER'S NOTE	Congratulations! You have completed the Sonday System 1 beginner program.
CHECK FOR MASTERY	Use Mastery Check 36, on the following page, to check progress.

Mastery Check for Reading
Use after Level 36

Using the Sonday System 1 Learning Plan format, incorporate Mastery Check for Reading in the 3. Read Words section. Have the Learner read the words aloud. Time limit is 30 seconds. If fewer than 90% of the words are read accurately, teach two more sessions and give Form B during the 3. Read Words section of the third session. Alternate Forms A and B at every third session until the Learner reaches 90%.

HELPER'S NOTE	Both Form A and B contain the same words but in a different order to avoid memorization of the sequence and require the Learner to read each word.

Have the student read the test from the Word Book, p. 149.

Reading Level 36 – Form A

chopstick	stewing	wishbone	brewing
flight	might	brighter	fighting
steaming	stage	bleacher	hinge
choice	boyscout	prance	voucher
couch	clearing	pounding	year

Reading Level 36 – Form B

steaming	stage	prance	voucher
choice	year	pounding	boyscout
brewing	wishbone	couch	clearing
fighting	brighter	stewing	chopsticks
might	bleacher	hinge	flight

Count the number of words correctly read and multiply by 5 to obtain the percentage correct or use the Conversion Chart below.

CONVERSION CHART

# Correct	%	# Correct	%	# Correct	%
1	5%	8	40%	15	75%
2	10%	9	45%	16	80%
3	15%	10	50%	17	85%
4	20%	11	55%	18	90%
5	25%	12	60%	19	95%
6	30%	13	65%	20	100%
7	35%	14	70%		

The Learner should have 90% accuracy on the this test and 85% accuracy on the Spelling Mastery Check before moving to the next level.

Mastery Check for Spelling
Use after Level 36

Dictate the following words, reading down the columns. Repeat the words if necessary, but don't help the Learner make corrections. The goal is to determine what has been learned and how well the Learner can spell independently.

switch	stew	shout	could
thaw	dredge	prince	pinch
soap	clear	smarter	drift
moist	bright	stage	trace
teach	boost	stuffing	forge

If 17 of the 20 words have been correctly spelled proceed to the next Level.

If four or more words are misspelled categorize the errors in the columns below by marking the letter or letters which represent the correct spelling. For example:

If	teach	is spelled as	teech	mark ea
If	stew	is spelled as	stoo	mark ew
If	bright	is spelled as	brite	mark igh
If	prince	is spelled as	prins	mark soft c

Errors	Word Book page	Errors	Word Book page	Errors	Word Book page
fszl □	27	ar □	62	aw □	104
sh □	24	oo □	67	oi □	104
s blends □	36	VCe □	71	oa □	105
l blends □	39,40	er □	96	soft c □	109
r blends □	43,44	-st,-nd,-nt □	74,75	soft g □	109
ch □	51	-mp,-sk, -ft □	75,76	ea □	113
or □	53	-tch □	99	ew □	114
th □	56	-dge □	99	ear □	114
ing □	95			igh □	118
				ou □	118
				could □	Sight Word

When you have identified the letters/sounds that need more practice, you may reuse Levels 34 – 36 or you may create Personalized Learning Plans following the instructions on the next two pages. The Word Book pages listed above will provide lists of words to use in creating learning plans. After at least four practice Sessions give this test again.

Creating A Personal Learning Plan

Using the form on the following page, construct a Personal Learning Plan to practice words and sounds that were missed in the Mastery Check along with words that have been mastered.

READ SOUNDS

- Use Sound Cards.
- Review all sounds that have been taught. Do this at every Session.

SPELL SOUNDS

- Use known sounds. Include those missed in the Mastery Check.
- Dictate 10 review sounds in 2 minutes or less at every Session.

READ WORDS

- Use Word Cards or Word Book lists that have been introduced.
- Read review words for 5 minutes at every Session.

SPELL WORDS

- Use words from the Word Cards or the Word Book that have been practiced. Include words that reinforce the sounds spelled incorrectly on the Mastery Check.
- Use sentences from the Word Book or create your own using words and sounds that have been taught.

READ ALOUD

- Use a Book to read, Reading Strips, or Board Game.

1 READ SOUNDS — 2 MIN.

- Review Sound Cards _____

2 SPELL SOUNDS — 2 MIN.

___ ___ ___ ___ ___ ___ ___ ___ ___ ___ ___ ___ ___

3 READ WORDS — 5 MIN.

- Word Book page _____
- Word Cards _____

4 SPELL WORDS — 7 MIN.

1. _____ _____ _____ _____ _____
2. _____ _____ _____ _____ _____
3. _____ _____ _____ _____ _____
4. _____ _____ _____ _____ _____
5. _____ _____ _____ _____ _____

- Dictate phrases or sentences

1. _____
2. _____

- Learner reads words and sentences just written.

5 READ ALOUD — 10 MIN.

Book to read

Reading Strip

Board Game

<u>Alphabet Strip</u> A long narrow strip of heavy paper inscribed with the letters of the alphabet for practice identifying, saying, sounding, sequencing, and tracing the letters.

<u>Audio Tape</u> A collection of original songs with bouncy music designed to reinforce language activities.
    <u>Alphabet Song</u> A musical alphabet with the sounds of the letters clearly separated.
    <u>Rhyming Song</u> Rhyming words set to music.
    <u>Beginning Sounds</u> Recognizing and repeating just the beginning sound of a word provides a foundation for spelling words.
    <u>Combining Words</u> Combining two small words to make one compound word is a foundation skill for sounding and blending words.
    <u>Dividing Words</u> Dividing a compound word into two short words is a foundation skill for spelling.

<u>Auditory</u> The learning modality or pathway that involves hearing and listening.

<u>NerfBall</u> A NerfBall or any soft ball that can be used in the Ball Toss Game.

<u>Ball Toss Game</u> This activity combines listening, segmenting and identifying sounds with movement. It builds language while providing a fun physical break.

<u>Base Word</u> The root word to which prefixes and suffixes may be added.

<u>Board Game</u> Two games are included to add interest and fun into practicing reading words. The rules for the games are written on the game board.

<u>Book to Read</u> Oral reading is an important part of every session. If your Learner can not read a book to you, spend a few minutes reading aloud to the Learner. As soon as possible, the Learner should be reading at the end of each Session.

<u>Cards</u> There are 14 decks of cards including Sound Cards and word flashcards to be used for drill and for games.
    <u>Sound Cards</u> are the drill cards for sounds. Letters are on one side, a picture and word example on the reverse. They are numbered in the order of introduction. 52 cards.
    <u>Gray Blend Cards</u> are drill cards for isolated blends. They are numbered in order of introduction.
    <u>Pink</u> Cards with consonant-vowel-consonant (CVC) words with short <u>a</u>
    <u>Blue</u> CVC words with short <u>i</u> - 27 cards.
    <u>Green</u> CVC words with short <u>o</u> - 27 cards.
    <u>Yellow</u> CVC words with short <u>u</u> - 27 cards.
    <u>Purple</u> CVC words with short <u>e</u> - 27 cards.
    <u>Orange</u> Words with <u>ay</u> and <u>ee</u> - 27 cards.
    <u>Tan 1</u> Words with beginning blends, <u>s</u> blends - 27 cards.
    <u>Tan 2</u> Words with beginning blends, <u>l</u> blends - 27 cards.
    <u>Tan 3</u> Words with beginning blends, <u>r</u> blends - 27 cards.
    <u>Gold</u> Words with ending blends - 27 cards.
    <u>Light Blue</u> Words with the vowel-consonant-e pattern (VCe) - 27 cards.
    <u>Red</u> Sight words are non-phonetic words that can't be sounded out. They are numbered in the order of introduction. - 27 cards.

<u>Consonant</u> A letter or symbol representing a sound. All letters in the alphabet are either consonants or vowels. The consonants in our alphabet are b c d f g h j k l m n p q r s t v w x y z.

Definitions and Descriptions

Consonant Blends A consonant blend consists of two consonants that blend together either at the beginning or end of a word. Examples: <u>st</u>op or sta<u>mp</u>.

CVC Words Words that follow the consonant-vowel-consonant pattern. Examples: pat, dim.

Key Words Words and pictures on the back of the Sound Cards which provide a memory key to the sound of a letter.
   For example, the key word for the letter 'b' is 'boy'.

Kinesthetic The learning modality or pathway that involves feeling with large motor movement. Example: Skywriting or other large writing medium.

Learning Plan Book This plan, written for each PreReading and Reading Level, provides a variety of activities and detailed step-by-step
   directions for teaching your Learner to read and spell

Letter Tactile Cards Tracing cards with raised and textured letters, starting points and directional arrows.

Levels There are five PreReading Levels and thirty-six Reading Levels. Each Level provides a complete review of everything that has been
   taught and introduces new sounds, rules or concepts. At each Reading Level the Learner will be asked to read and spell sounds, read
   and spell words, and read and spell phrases, sentences or paragraphs. More than one Session is needed to complete a Level. There
   are more activities and more practice materials at each Level than your Learner can complete in one Session.

Lower Case Small letters, not capital letters, in either printing or cursive. Examples: a b c d e f g

Mastery Check A twenty word spelling dictation used after every third Level. Check for mastery to measure progress, to identify letters,
   sounds, and rules that need additional practice and to determine whether or not to proceed to the next level.

Multisensory Reinforcement Practice using seeing, hearing, and touching to involve all pathways of learning to read and spell.

New material New sounds, rules or concepts are introduced at every Level. Only one new sound or concept should be introduced at
   any Session. It is not necessary or advisable to introduce new material at every Session.

PreReading Levels The five PreReading Levels are designed to provide a foundation for teaching reading and spelling.
   The PreReading Levels include:
        1. Learning the alphabet   2. Developing listening skills.   3. Printing letters
        4. Playing with sound puzzles.   5. Converting letter to sound.
   Work through them as quickly as possible, but take as much time as you need. Some children in the first grade may be able to do
   all of the activities while some middle elementary children may not have these basics in place. The foundation or readiness skills
   should be in place for successful reading and spelling.

Reading Marker A marker for the Learner to place under the word or sentence being read.

Root Word The base word to which prefixes and suffixes may be added.

Reading Strip The strip of phrases or sentences to be used with the Reading Window.

® Reminder to helper.

<u>Reading Window</u> Thread the Reading Strip through the Reading Window to show one phrase or sentence or one pair of sentences for oral reading.

<u>Sand tray</u> Flat tray with a shallow layer of sand for tracing sounds and words to reinforce learning of letters or words by touching or feeling. See the video demonstration. Other devices for encouraging touch reinforcement for printing letters and numbers could include finger paint, shaving cream, a carpet sample, chalkboard with chalk or a wet foam brush, magic slate, or paper with crayons or markers.

<u>Sessions</u> Sessions should last about 30-40 minutes. Each Level can involve two to ten Sessions, depending on the success your Learner is experiencing. Beginning Levels may go quickly because the Learner knows most of the material but progress will slow as unfamiliar material is introduced. Always begin a Session with

      1. Read Sounds   2. Spell Sounds   3. Read Words   4. Spell Words

<u>Slashes</u> The marks on either side of a letter, /b/, indicating that the sound, not the letter name, should be dictated.

<u>Sound Puzzles</u> Auditory activities and games that involve listening to sounds, words and parts of words and manipulating the pieces.

<u>Suffix</u> An ending attached after a base or root word, for example, '-ing' in 'parking' or '-er' in 'farmer'.

<u>Tactile</u> The learning modality or pathway that builds motor memory by involving feeling or touching. Examples: writing, tracing.

<u>Time Recommendations</u> The recommendations are guidelines. Practice all skills during each Session. Don't expect to finish all of the suggested activities in any category within the time recommendations. Alternate activities are provided so that there is variety and fun in the learning Sessions.

<u>Touch Spelling</u> Segment words into sounds or syllables using the fingers on the non-writing hand. After teaching the sounds in isolation, it is helpful for the Learner to have a strategy to divide a word into separate, recognizable sounds. Watch the video for a demonstration.

<u>Tracing</u> A multi-sensory strategy that cements letter forms and words into motor memory. Using the first two fingers of writing hand to trace in a sand tray, on a table, on paper or any textured surface will anchor images in long term memory where they are easily retrieved.

<u>Transparency</u> A clear plastic sheet to place over worksheets to keep the worksheets unmarked for future use. Transparencies may be cleaned by rinsing under the faucet with cool water.

<u>Transparency pen</u> A felt-tipped pen with washable ink used to write on transparencies.

<u>Upper Case</u> Capital letters, in either printing or cursive. Examples: A B C D

<u>Visual</u> The learning modality or pathway that involves seeing.

<u>Vowel</u> A letter or symbol representing a sound. All letters in the alphabet are either vowels or consonants. The vowels in our alphabet are a e i o u and sometimes y.

<u>VCe</u> Words following the vowel-consonant-silent e pattern. Examples: game, time.

<u>Word Book</u> A book of word lists, phrases, sentences and worksheets, organized to teach and practice specific sounds and provide a cumulative review of all sounds introduced.

Quick Reference to English Language Rules

Sound	Level Introduced	Rule
a	1	Short a is found at the beginning or middle of a word.
ai	27	Use ai to spell long /a/ in the middle of words, usually before an n or l. Examples: rain, rail, train, trail, main.
aw	32	aw is usually found at the end of a word or sometimes followed by n or l. Examples: law, raw, claw, dawn, lawn, crawl.
ay	6	ay is always used at the end of a word.
c		c is the first choice for /k/ at the beginning of a word.
c	33	c has the soft sound, /s/, when followed by e, i or y.
ck	13	Use ck to spell /k/ after a short vowel. Examples: black, stick, lock. Use k at the end after a consonant, a long vowel or a double vowel. Examples: pink, cork, bike, soak, peak.
dge	31	Use dge to spell /j/ after a short vowel. Examples: badge, bridge, lodge, fudge. Use ge at the end after a consonant, a long vowel or a double vowel. Examples: barge, plunge, rage, gouge.
e	9	Short e is found at the beginning or middle of a word.
e	25	Silent e on the end of a word usually makes the preceding vowel long or say its name. Examples: same, these, time, hope, cute.
ee	8	ee is the first choice for the long sound of e in the middle of a word.
er	30	er is found in the middle of a word or at the end as a suffix.
ew	34	The first choice for spelling /oo/ at the end of a word is ew. Examples: new, blew, flew.
fszl	12	Double the final f, s, z, or l in short words after a single vowel. Examples: pass, cuff, buzz, will.
g	33	The letter g has the soft sound /j/ when followed by e, i or y. Examples: gentle, ginger, gym, fringe.
i	3	Short i is found at the beginning or middle of a word.
igh	35	igh is usually at the end of a word or followed by t. Examples: high, sight, might.

Sound	Level Introduced	Rule
k	24	k is the first choice for /k/ at the end of a word after a consonant, a long vowel or a double vowel. Examples: pink, cork, bike, soak, peak.
o	4	Short o is found at the beginning or middle of a word.
oa	32	oa is usually found in the middle of short words. Examples: soap, load, toast.
oi	32	oi is found at the beginning or middle of a word. Examples: coin, boil, moist.
oo	29	The first choice for spelling /oo/ in the middle of a word is oo. Examples: soon, smooth, loop.
ou	35	The first choice for spelling /ow/ in the middle of a word is ou. Examples: shout, found, mouth.
ow	27	The first choice for spelling long /o/ at the end of a word is ow. When ow is not at the end of a word, it is often followed by n. Examples: show, blow, flown, thrown.
ow	29	ow pronounced /ow/ as in cow is usually at the end of a word or followed by n or l. Examples: how, now, down, clown, growl, prowl.
oy	23	oy is usually at the end of a word.
qu	14	the letter q is always followed by u and one or more vowels. Examples: quit, quack, queen.
tch	31	Use tch to spell /ch/ after a short vowel. Examples: catch, pitch, notch, clutch. Use ch at the end after a consonant or a double vowel. Examples: pinch, torch, teach, couch.
th	21	th has two sounds one voiced on unvoiced. Examples: thick, thin, that, those.
u	7	Short u is found at the beginning or middle of a word.
v, w, x		The letters v, w, and x are never doubled.
wh	23	The letters wh always come at the beginning of a word.
y	18	When y comes at the end of a short word, it has the sound of long /i/. Examples: cry, fly, by.

Sonday System 1 – Scope and Sequence

Level	Sounds and Cards	Non-phonetic Words
PreRdg 5	s, t, b, m, l, d, n, p, k, j, v, z, f, c, g, r, h	
1	a (at)	
2	a (mixed)	
3	i	
4	o	
5	x	a, the
6	ay	to, do, is
7	u	
8	ee	I, of, and
9	e	
10	w, y	
11	sh	
12	f s z l	
13	-ck	
14	qu	you, from
15	st, sp, sm, sn, sc, sw	
16	bl, cl, fl, pl, gl, sl	
17	cr, tr, fr, dr, br, pr, gr	
18	final long vowels: y (long i), e, o	are, was, who, what
19	ch	
20	or, all	
21	th	your, said, were
22	-ing, -ang, -ong, -ung	
23	oy, ar, wh	one, only, once, does
24	-ink, -ank, -onk, -unk oo (soon)	
25	v-consonant-e	two, four, done, goes
26	-st, -nd, -nt, -mp, -sk, -ft	where, there
27	ow (blow) ai	gone, don't, they, some, come
28	compound words, -lt, -lk, -sp, -ct	says, want, any, been, their
29	ow (owl) oo (book)	
30	suffixes -ing, -er	
31	-tch, -dge	have, give, live
32	aw, oa, oi	
33	soft c, soft g	could, would, should, very
34	ea, ew, ear	
35	igh, ou	
36	review	